Praise for Tam
and *Fait*

MW00416073

"Much has been written about the young white exodus from evangelical religion. Rarely have we been invited to journey alongside young evangelicals of color. Tamice Spencer-Helms takes readers by the hand and walks them through her exodus and liberation. We witness the scales falling from her eyes and see with her, for the first time, that the white evangelical waters she once found respite within are actually filled with the rotting bodies of theology and discipleship stunted and killed by White Jesus. Walk with Tamice through each stage of her healing and transformation, and encounter unleavened faith. This is a worthy read, indeed."

—Lisa Sharon Harper, President and Founder of Freedom Road, LLC and author of several books, including *The Very Good Gospel* and *Fortune: How Race Broke My Family And The World—And How To Repair It All*

"Tamice is an incredibly important voice as someone who lives faith at the intersection of practitioner and theologian. Her reflections on historical events that have shaped this emerging generation is a gift to anyone who mentors young people of any racial background, since these events have shaped our ecosystem."

—Rev. Sandra Maria Van Opstal, Founder of Chasing Justice

"We all contend with a wilderness and on that journey, it's necessary to choose what we consume. In *Faith Unleavened*, Tamice showed me a path I hadn't seen and gave me nuggets of a better way to do community and life with one another. I've still so much to learn. Join me in the wilderness."

—Seth Price, host of the *Can I Say This at Church?* podcast

"I learn so much from listening to stories unlike my own. In this memoir of evolving faith, Tamice bravely invites us into a journey that is tender but unflinching, heavy with grief and suffused with hope. I am challenged by the ways we disagree with one another, and even more challenged by the ways we agree."

—Gregory Coles, author of *Single, Gay, Christian* and *No Longer Strangers*

"In *Faith Unleavened*, Tamice Spencer-Helms vulnerably provides us with her exile experience in white evangelicalism and her courageous exodus out of it. Doing so, she offers a gift for the rest of us, inviting everyone to let go of White Jesus so we can encounter the living, liberating, and unleavened Bread of God. Read this book!"

—Drew G. I. Hart, Associate Professor of Theology at Messiah University, author of *Who Will Be A Witness?*, and co-host of the *InVerse* Podcast

"We all need fellow sojourners on our path to a more beautiful, just world. Tamice Spencer-Helms is an ideal guide for those seeking to leave behind faith narratives of exclusion, violence, greed, sexism, exploitation, and racism rooted in white supremacy for narratives of reconciliation, inclusion, nonviolence, generosity, equality, and sustainability. Spencer-Helms displays a powerful, honest, and clarion voice in *Faith Unleavened*. This book is a must-read for all who care about the role of faith in a world seeking justice."

—Doug Pagitt, pastor, author, activist, Executive Director of Vote Common Good

"Tamice Spencer-Helms guides us through the wilderness of a Black woman contorting herself to a white Jesus and into freedom as a Black woman fully seen and loved by herself and Jesus. Spencer-Helms shares her doubts and the obstacles to decolonizing faith with a vulnerability and honesty that made me flinch. She powerfully names how white supremacy gaslights all of us and she gives hope to those still on the journey."

—Kathy Khang, author of *Raise Your Voice*

"A faith cannot feed you until you have first wrestled with it and sat with the story it has yielded in your life. In *Faith Unleavened*, Tamice Spencer-Helms shares the story of her wrestling in the wilderness and the sustenance she found therein. May we all be courageous enough to trust God with our stories."

—Pastor Trey Ferguson, Founding President of Rebellion for Christ Ministries, co-host of the *Three Black Men* podcast

"Everyone should read Tamice's story. She describes how white supremacist beliefs in Christian organizations deepen pain and self-hatred for people of color, especially when they are trying to minister from those frameworks. She illustrates how both over-rationalism and over-emotionalism in white evangelical theology(ies) hinder trauma processing instead of helping. She shows how shallow understandings of God, people, and society cause more problems than they solve. But Tamice helps us glimpse the glory of Christ in the Black Church!"

—Mako Nagasawa, Founder & Executive Director of the Anástasis Center, author of *Abortion Policy and Christian Social Ethics in the United States*

"Tamice Spencer-Helms writes with honesty and courage about her confounding journey through white Evangelical Christianity. For the sake of future and current generations we need to listen and learn from her story. If you've ever felt betrayed by your faith or bamboozled by life, this book will inspire you to keep going. You matter, healing is possible, and together we can seek the love and justice of the kingdom of God."

—Mark Scandrette, teacher and author of
The Ninefold Path of Jesus: Hidden Wisdom of the Beatitudes

"Tamice beautifully takes us along her journey in and out of whiteness. By weaving in her personal story, world and church history, and current events she leads us into our own personal exploration of what our experiences with whiteness, White Jesus, anti-blackness, and the Church have been like. This book bears witness to the death-dealing ways of a system that refuses to see people but insists on the superiority of its ways, politics, songs, ideology, and theology. Tamice's journey out of the system gives me hope that redemption is possible—revolution is possible. So come on.... let's get us some unleavened bread and have ourselves a revolution!"

—Carol Ng'ang'a, Founder & Executive Director of Msingi Trust

"In this critical book, Tamice eloquently and painfully takes us on a journey through racial trauma and faith deconstruction, all while allowing the grace to sit with discomfort. She brings forth her own story in a way that is undeniably brilliant. Take your time with each section of this poignant writing."

—Robert Monson, Co-Director of Enfleshed,
co-host of the *Three Black Men* podcast

"To the image-bearers who have been told they were naked before and above being told they are Loved, let Tamice take your hand as a fellow sojourner of the wilderness in *Faith Unleavened*. Tamice sews history and scripture into a tapestry through the stitchwork of storytelling; inviting us into her painful, particular, and common experience as a Black woman in the white evangelical expression of Christianity. In this wilderness—I mean, right in the middle—Tamice sets an abundant table both for the collective and just for you. Here laughter and tears, sorrow and song beckon each of us to eat until we are full of the unleavened bread Jesus has provided."

—Nya Abernathy, Founder of The Dignity Effect, writer at *Of Earth & Of Stars*

"This is the story of leaving behind a controlling, small religion, and going on the hunt for a faith that is big enough to hold everyone and everything. Within these pages is a memoir of liberation...not just for Tamice but for all of us."

—Scott Hall, host of the *White People Work* podcast

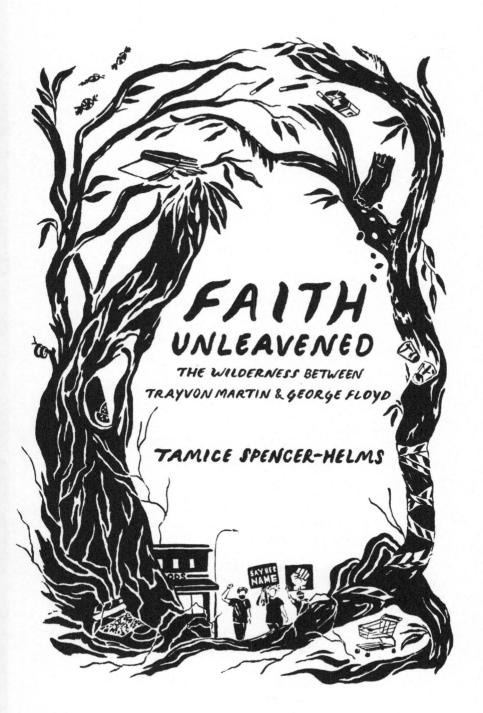

FAITH
UNLEAVENED
THE WILDERNESS BETWEEN
TRAYVON MARTIN & GEORGE FLOYD

TAMICE SPENCER-HELMS

Faith Unleavened: The Wilderness between Trayvon Martin and George Floyd
Copyright © by Tamice Spencer-Helms 2023.
All rights reserved.

Faith Unleavened: The Wilderness between Trayvon Martin and George Floyd published globally in 2023 by KTF Press LLC, 651 N Broad St, Suite 201, Middletown, Delaware 19709. No part of this book may be used or reproduced in any manner whatsoever without written permission except in the case of brief quotations embodied in critical articles and reviews.

Every effort has been made to obtain permission for pieces quoted or adapted in this work. If any required acknowledgements have been omitted, or any rights overlooked, it is unintentional. Please notify KTF Press LLC of any omission, and it will be rectified in future editions.

Paperback ISBN 978-1-7358337-2-9
E-book ISBN 978-1-7358337-3-6

Cover design and original illustration by Jacqueline Tam © 2023.

For Leah and Ellsworth,
Thank you for helping me make sense of it all.

For Harlym and Ellison,
You are the first fruits of my resurrection.

Table of Contents

Prologue

When they flipped his body over, the bright canary yellow blanket fell on the grass. His hoodie was damp because he'd been laying there a while, and it had been raining that night. He was wearing jeans and fresh Fusion Force 20s. The red, black, and white ones with the red strap and patterned flap. I recognized those Jordans because my brother has a pair. His fade was cut the same and his skin was a darkened caramel color too. It could have been my brother under that sheet. His 7-Eleven lighter along with the Skittles he'd bought his little brother were strewn on the lawn, and they found the AriZona iced tea a little bit later.[1]

I didn't sleep that night. I kept thinking about the shoes.

That Sunday when I went to church, we sang happy songs about God's goodness and glorious reign. No one talked about Trayvon, not even the pastor. We learned about joy and gladness the week the 911 recordings came out, and we prayed for revival in America during the rallies in Sanford, Florida.

In November of the same year Trayvon died, Jordan Davis was shot to death because a white man thought his music was

[1] Orlando Sentinel, ed., "Pictures: Evidence Photos Released in the Shooting Death of Trayvon Martin," *Orlando Sentinel,* May 17, 2012, https://www.orlandosentinel.com/news/trayvon-martin-george-zimmerman/os-pictures-evidence-photos-released-in-the-shooting-death-of-trayvon-martin-20120517-photogallery.html.

too loud,[2] and Rekia Boyd was shot in the head while standing with some friends. The off-duty officer carelessly fired shots over his shoulder into the group because he thought her friend's cell phone was a gun.[3] At church the day after the jury acquitted Trayvon's killer, they talked about how sad it was that the guy from *Glee* died. They didn't know anything about Trayvon. They didn't even know his name.

I felt a deep and nauseous sadness that grew more and more unbearable. I told my friends, but they didn't understand why I would be so upset about some "thug" in Florida being in the wrong place at the wrong time. Or why I was concerned about how many white people were on the jury of that other trial I'd been telling them about—the one where the boy stole the Snickers and died.

"His name was Trayvon, and he didn't steal," I told them. I didn't tell them about my brother, and I didn't tell them about his shoes. They didn't deserve to know.

Four months later, in the middle of the night, Renisha McBride was shot in the face with a 12-gauge pistol-grip Mossberg shotgun through a screen door on her neighbor's porch because she was knocking too loudly.[4] Eight months after that, in New York, Eric Garner was choked to death in broad daylight for selling individual Newport Kings that weren't in

---

[2] News Service of Florida, "Man Who Shot, Killed Jacksonville Teen Jordan Davis in 2012 Appeals to Florida Supreme Court," *Action News Jax*, December 13, 2019, https://www.actionnewsjax.com/news/local/man-who-shot-killed-jacksonville-teen-jordan-davis-2012-appeals-florida-supreme-court/AFERBGLA4NFZTCBK3ESWMGOBIA/.

[3] Taylor Lewis, "Police Officer Found Not Guilty in Death of Rekia Boyd," *Essence*, October 27, 2020, https://www.essence.com/news/police-officer-found-not-guilty-death-rekia-boyd/.

[4] Monica Davey, "Fatal Shooting of Black Woman Outside Detroit Stirs Racial Tensions," *The New York Times*, November 15, 2013, https://www.nytimes.com/2013/11/15/us/fatal-shooting-of-black-woman-outside-detroit-stirs-racial-tensions.html.

their original packaging[5]—the kind Rigby, my auntie, used to smoke. She called them "loosies." Eric told the officer he could not breathe, but it didn't matter.

In Ohio one month later, John Crawford was shot inside a Walmart for picking up a gun they sold in the store while his girlfriend gathered ingredients to make s'mores.[6] Michael Brown was shot six times and left lying face down in Ferguson, Mo., in August in the middle of the road. The officer let his body fry on the asphalt of his neighborhood for four hours in front of his mother's house.[7] Two days after that, Ezell Ford was shot in the back at close range. The officers who killed Ezell said they stopped him for "walking on the sidewalk at 65th Street."[8] Two months after that, Laquan McDonald was shot 16 times in 13 seconds. The officer said he was afraid for his life because of the folded pocketknife in Laquan's pocket.[9] The next month, a 12-year-old boy was shot in the torso for

[5] History.com Editors, ed., "Eric Garner Dies in NYPD Chokehold," History.com (A&E Television Networks, July 15, 2020), https://www.history.com/this-day-in-history/eric-garner-dies-nypd-chokehold.

[6] John Swaine, "Video Shows John Crawford's Girlfriend Aggressively Questioned after Ohio Police Shot Him Dead in Walmart," The Guardian (Guardian News and Media, December 14, 2014), https://www.theguardian.com/us-news/2014/dec/14/john-crawford-girlfriend-questioned-walmart-police-shot-dead?CMP=share_btn_tw.

[7] Julie Bosman and Joseph Goldstein, "Timeline for a Body: 4 Hours in the Middle of a Ferguson Street," The New York Times, August 23, 2014, https://www.nytimes.com/2014/08/24/us/michael-brown-a-bodys-timeline-4-hours-on-a-ferguson-street.html#:~:text=For%20at%20least%20four%20hours,for%20two%20weeks%20of%20unrest.

[8] Kate Mather, Richard Winton, Ruben Vives, LA Times, "Ezell Earl Ford, 25," The Homicide Report, Los Angeles Times, August 11, 2014, https://homicide.latimes.com/post/ezell-ford/.

[9] Kori Rumore and Chad Yoder, "Minute by Minute: How Jason Van Dyke Shot Laquan McDonald," Chicago Tribune, September 17, 2019, https://www.chicagotribune.com/news/laquan-mcdonald/ct-jason-vandyke-laquan-mcdonald-timeline-htmlstory.html.

playing with a toy gun in the park.[10] He died the next day. His name was Tamir Rice. In April of the next year, Freddie Gray's spinal cord was snapped in half while he was being transported by police for possessing what they referred to as an illegal switchblade; they didn't buckle him in when they drove him away.[11] In November, Jamar Clark was shot in the head while handcuffed,[12] and Akai Gurley was shot to death while walking down the stairs.[13] Walter Scott was shot dead in the back by an officer who lied in his report.[14] Just across the border of that town, only two months later, nine Black men and women were massacred in their own church during Bible study.[15]

Alton Sterling was selling CDs out of his trunk at a corner store in Baton Rouge when he was pinned to the ground and shot five times in the chest at close range.[16] And the very next day, the entire world watched live as Philando Castile bled to

[10] Jamiel Lynch and Christina Carrega, "Justice Department Won't Pursue Charges against Officers in Tamir Rice Shooting," CNN, December 30, 2020, https://www.cnn.com/2020/12/29/us/tamir-rice-shooting-no-federal-charges/index.html.

[11] Amelia McDonell-Parry, "Death of Freddie Gray: 5 Things You Didn't Know," *Rolling Stone*, June 2, 2020, https://www.rollingstone.com/culture/culture-features/death-of-freddie-gray-5-things-you-didnt-know-129327/.

[12] Sara Sidner, Steve Almasy, and Joshua Berlinger, "Jamar Clark Shooting: Witness Says He Was in Handcuffs," CNN, November 22, 2015, https://www.cnn.com/2015/11/21/us/minneapolis-jamar-clark-police-shooting.

[13] Sarah Maslin Nir, "Officer Peter Liang Convicted in Fatal Shooting of Akai Gurley in Brooklyn," *The New York Times*, February 12, 2016, https://www.nytimes.com/2016/02/12/nyregion/officer-peter-liang-convicted-in-fatal-shooting-of-akai-gurley-in-brooklyn.html.

[14] Hannah Grabenstein, "Walter Scott," PBS, December 17, 2017, https://www.pbs.org/newshour/tag/walter-scott.

[15] Associated Press, "Supreme Court Rejects Appeal from Dylann Roof, Who Killed 9 People in a Black Church," PBS, October 11, 2022, https://www.pbs.org/newshour/nation/supreme-court-rejects-appeal-from-dylann-roof-who-killed-9-people-in-a-black-church.

[16] Catherine E. Shoichet, Joshua Berlinger, and Steve Almasy, "Alton Sterling Shooting: Second Video of Deadly Encounter Emerges," CNN, July 7, 2016, https://www.cnn.com/2016/07/06/us/baton-rouge-shooting-alton-sterling/index.html.

death in front of his 4-year-old daughter and his girlfriend. He was shot seven times while sitting in the passenger seat. He was wearing his seatbelt.[17]

But still the pastor didn't say anything.

"Numb" is not the right word because it was sharper than that. "Angry" won't suffice either because it was deeper. It was as if the world was spinning, and I could not find my balance. With every hashtag, the crack in the toxic foundations of my faith grew wider. Where do you run when the only person you can turn to is White Jesus? I could not breathe. I could not sing another damn song about joy. I didn't know it then, but I was fellowshipping with the 81% of white evangelicals who voted for Donald Trump, and there was leaven in the bread.[18] How could they be so oblivious to the issue at hand? How could they not see it? Why did they argue with me so much about it? Why did *I* have to calm down?

They were convinced all those who had been killed had done something wrong, something to deserve being gunned down like beasts with no family, no future, and no dignity. Why were all the pictures of the slain so dark and thuggish? Why were all the murderers in uniforms and family photos?

The anguish was unbearable. It was the culmination of so many things I'd ignored for so many years. How many Black bodies had to drop before they cared? Didn't Jesus care? Why didn't they know any of their names? And why did all the

---

[17] Ralph Ellis and Bill Kirkos, "Officer Who Shot Philando Castile Found Not Guilty on All Counts," CNN, June 17, 2017, https://www.cnn.com/2017/06/16/us/philando-castile-trial-verdict.

[18] Martínez, Jessica, and Gregory A. Smith. "How the Faithful Voted: A Preliminary 2016 Analysis." Pew Research Center, August 27, 2020. https://www.pewresearch.org/fact-tank/2016/11/09/how-the-faithful-voted-a-preliminary-2016-analysis/.

GoFundMe money go toward George Zimmerman's bail instead of Trayvon's burial? Deep inside I knew something was happening to me, and I knew it was the beginning of the end. Of what? I didn't know. I hoped it wasn't my faith, but I didn't have the energy to fight it. I couldn't see Jesus through the pile of dead Black bodies anyway. I spent the three years after Trayvon died in perpetual despair.

It felt like there was trauma in my bones. Like I was carrying the pain and the weight of the entire struggle for freedom and dignity, and I couldn't decide if I wanted to be free. At the same time, this pain gave me a sort of strength, and it began to lift me. Right as it did, Donald J. Trump was coming down an escalator to announce his run for the presidency.

And I began seeing red.

Trayvon Martin, his shoes, and the trial of George Zimmerman were responsible for the beginning of my exodus from toxic, white Christianity. Before that, my peers in the white churches I attended routed their racist attitudes through religious beliefs and backed them with biblical authority, which made them harder for me to detect or resist. But when Trayvon died, it was the straw that broke the camel's back. Religion was no longer an adequate obfuscation. George Zimmerman's story just didn't add up.

Initially, Zimmerman saw Trayvon walking through a gated community and began following because he thought Trayvon seemed suspicious. Zimmerman followed in his car, and then on foot when Trayvon turned off the sidewalk to go through a backyard. Zimmerman even ignored police who told him to leave the teenager alone and let them handle it.[19] Acting as self-appointed gatekeeper that night, he saw a young Black boy and thought, "*Intruder*." Trayvon was 17, unarmed, and minding his own business.

My friends didn't budge when I tried to talk to them about it. It was sad, they told me, but I needed to trust that Jesus was on the throne and remind myself what Paul said in Romans 13 about respecting authority. But what was dangerous about a boy in a hoodie? What is threatening about a bag of candy? What authority did Zimmerman carry? Even still, they were positive they were not racists. How could they be, when they were friends with me? They were just being objective, radical for the truth, swayed only by facts.

I reeled as the list of hashtags grew and the people around me did not. Jesus couldn't be this cold and unfeeling. There had to be a way to love both God and my neighbor with a clear conscience and common sense. It had to be possible to love and follow Jesus in a way that would let me sleep at night. There had to be an answer for the carnage and something stronger than the rage. There had to be a way to love the Lord and breathe. I could not breathe. I didn't need Jesus to be on the throne, I needed Jesus to come down here. I could no longer worship a god whose love couldn't break through yellow caution tape. I could not negotiate any longer with a god who could not meet me on blood-soaked asphalt next to shell casings, evidence markers, and white chalk. But I did not know where to find that God. At the same time, I had the gross realization that

---

[19] Adam Weinstein and Mark Follman, "The Trayvon Martin Killing, Explained," *Mother Jones*, March 18, 2012, https://www.motherjones.com/politics/2012/03/what-happened-trayvon-martin-explained/.

my only purpose in the lives of some of my colleagues in ministry was to sanction their racist attitudes with my silence born of self-preservation. I held my tongue in the name of unity among believers, but they never held theirs. They made ignorant and infuriating comments without any hesitation or care for the ways their opinions did violence to my soul. I fell into a deep depression and began to let tequila do the work that the Spirit once did.

The murders of Trayvon Martin and George Floyd took place at either end of a number of messy, painful, glorious, beautiful, and liberative things that happened in my life and theology, which are the focus of this book. Trayvon's death caused the upheaval of everything I knew and believed. As everything came crashing down around me, I was left with mere fragments of the faith that had motivated every major decision I'd made up to that point.

The devastation defined me for a time and led me into a dark and lonely place until the silence from God broke one day in 2015. That word from God gave me the courage and permission I needed to begin extracting the poison from the Christianity I had adopted. If Jesus was the bread of life, then there was something else making me sick and I needed to figure out what it was. I learned it wasn't the bread; it was the leaven of whiteness.

May 25, 2020, the day a police officer murdered George Floyd, was a wake-up call for a lot of white people, but I couldn't at that point call any of them friends. I'd lost so many of them along the wayside of the acquittals and non-indictments in the years that followed Trayvon's death. By that point, I'd given up bickering over confederate flags and monuments and trying to help them recognize how atrocious their justifications for brown children in cages were. Too much had transpired, and it was too late for their apologies to have any bearing on my well-being or my tolerance for White Jesus.

I broke when George Floyd was killed, but I did not break the same. The systems hadn't changed, but I was different, and that changed the nature of the sting. As the world witnessed the horrors and toxicity of the yeast of whiteness, I loved myself, my Blackness, and the truth enough to find refuge and solidarity in Jesus, the author and perfector of a new, *unleavened* faith.

FAITH UNLEAVENED

10

I
PART ONE

FAITH UNLEAVENED

Walking Back

It had been three years since Trayvon was killed. I was living in Atlanta, Georgia, working in full-time college ministry. And I was dying. I had enough experience to do *student* discipleship on fumes and autopilot. But the extent of my Christianity at the time was to take shots of Patrón and walk to the little church near my apartment complex for communion.

I loved the sounds of the city, hearing and feeling the thump of trap music as cars rolled by. The air was refreshing and carried the voices of friends having brunch and neighbors calling to one another. Every week I waited until most of the congregants were gone before sneaking inside. The pews were wooden, and they made a creaking sound when I sat down. The communion station was self-service, so the elements were always sitting there on a table in the back of the sanctuary. That was the perfect placement. No one spoke to me; I didn't speak to them. I just climbed the stairs, opened the doors, and took my seat. I let the air conditioning cool me off and breathed the sweet smell of store-bought Danishes and drip coffee. Once I caught my breath or the liquid courage kicked in (whichever came first), I would walk up to the table and take communion the same way I did when I was young. I broke the bread and placed it on the tip of my tongue until it became soggy, then sat back down on the creaky pew before I took the cup to my lips.

I drank the wine in a way that washed the bread down with it. I concentrated on the feeling and pretended it was coating my heart and settling deep inside me. I'd think about all the years that led to me sitting in the back of that random church, tipsy and tired. I drank to quiet the noise of Divine silence and despondency that so often accompanied the walks to and from what I now refer to as my Tequila Sunrise Services.

Most days it felt as though I did not have anything left to say to God, and I was too scared to listen for the Spirit's voice. I couldn't trust anything anymore and listening prayer felt awkward, like being trapped in an elevator with someone you used to know. Every time I closed my eyes to talk to God, I panicked. I felt robbed of my favorite place, a place that was so special to me, a place I'd cultivated over the years that made up my twenties. That place was no longer safe. It was violent and scary and chaotic and loud. My heart was rent with anguish and disillusionment.

But I couldn't unsee Jesus. I couldn't pretend I'd never encountered him in the scriptures or that he never fascinated me. I still loved the gospel narratives because they'd provoked countless conversations with the Divine that had melted me, moved me, and molded me. The scriptures always found me in places I didn't expect the words of life or light to be. I couldn't lie to myself or anyone else about that.

But now Bible reading was an anxiety attack waiting to happen. When I turned inward to commune with God it felt akin to standing in the middle of Atlanta's interstate during rush hour. There was traffic in my very soul, and movement toward any sort of hope or peace was stop-and-go. It was all slipping away, and I was losing my grip on hope. I felt violated, lied to, and sad. The Voice I'd come to know so well, to recognize so quickly, was drowning underneath all the hashtags, press conferences, and tweets from the Republican presidential nominee.

I knew what I had been taught to do: turn it off, shut it down, do a social media fast. But it wasn't the news that was bothering me. I was nauseated by the hypocrisy of the 81% of white evangelicals who voted for Trump.[20] Up until the inauguration, they were still in close enough proximity to really devastate me. I thought about all the years I'd spent searching for Jesus and trying to figure out what it meant to know him. I reminisced about all the tears and spiritual experiences that were so real I couldn't explain them away. I thought about all the people I'd led in ministry and all the talks I'd given that must have caused so much harm to students who trusted me because I was asking them to believe a gospel that wasn't actually good news. Sitting there alone on that creaky, wooden pew, my heart felt frozen as if I were witnessing a tragedy but I couldn't even tell which way was up, let alone save myself.

I went back and forth between missing Jesus and resenting him. I loved him and I doubted his existence. I identified as an atheist at least twice a week and still resorted to certain worship musicians when days were particularly dark.

I had no idea where I was when it came to Christianity, but for some reason I never stopped taking communion. It was special to me. It was what I remembered most from my earliest days in church. I was drawn and driven to the mystery and

[20] Martínez, Jessica, and Gregory A. Smith. "How the Faithful Voted: A Preliminary 2016 Analysis." Pew Research Center, August 27, 2020. https://www.pewresearch.org/fact-tank/2016/11/09/how-the-faithful-voted-a-preliminary-2016-analysis/.

tenderness of it. It felt like home in a way. It held space for me. Every week was the same as I wept and whispered some variation of the phrases: *I think I still believe. I don't know how. I don't know what to do. I don't know what happened. I still love you. I can't do this. Please don't make me go back.*

There were so many reasons to stop going to this church, and I always dreaded the walk back home. I lived on the fourth floor, my building had no elevator, and it was hot. And yet these Sundays evolved into a ritual that lasted the entire three years I lived in that apartment. It had been three years of wondering, wandering, and rote sacraments. Then it happened one day on my way back home from communion. I was just arriving at the steps to my apartment when the silence suddenly broke.

It was just one word at first:

Remember.

Then a sentence:

I'm the Bread of Life, Tamice, remember.

The voice was soft, but it shook me. That's how I knew it was him.

Eat *This* Bread

They should take some of the blood and smear it on the two doorposts and on the beam over the door of the houses in which they are eating. That same night they should eat the meat roasted over the fire. They should eat it along with unleavened bread and bitter herbs ... This day will be a day of remembering for you. You will observe it as a festival to the Lord. You will observe it in every generation as a regulation for all time. You will eat unleavened bread for seven days. On the first day you must remove yeast from your houses because anyone who eats leavened bread anytime during those seven days will be cut off from Israel.

—Exodus 12:7-8, 14-15 (CEB)

According to the scriptures, the foundational event establishing Hebrew peoplehood is their exodus from slavery in Egypt. God's sovereign response, rescue, and redemption is the prototype of salvation and liberation throughout the rest of the Bible. The aspects of this story we typically highlight have to do with the magnificent signs and wonders that God does through

Moses when he confronts Pharaoh and frees his people. Exodus has rightly served as fodder for many generations and communities as they grappled with enslavement, oppression, and deliverance. It has helped me make sense of my experiences from Trayvon Martin's death to George Floyd's, and all the Black lives that should've mattered in between. But the most helpful framework that emerged from the story for me was not plague and pestilence. It was Unleavened Bread.

In the ancient near Eastern context, bread was a common metaphor to illustrate the sustenance of life. Ancient Egypt held a monopoly on grain and was known as the breadbasket of the Mediterranean world.[21] Even today, Egyptians call bread "Aish Baladi." Baladi means traditional or authentic in English, but the word "Aish" is literally translated "life," which is how Egyptians have perceived bread since ancient times.[22] Everyone, including slaves, depended on the bread of Egypt. The Ancient Egyptians developed the idea of leaven and were the first civilization to add it to their dough.[23] The night before God delivers the Hebrews from bondage, he says to leave it out of their bread.[24]

Baking unleavened bread and the famous preparation of the sacrificial lamb were the only parts of the events leading up to the Exodus that required the full participation of the

---

[21] Joshua J. Mark, "Ancient Egyptian Agriculture," *World History Encyclopedia* (https://www.worldhistory.org#organization, November 28, 2022), https://www.worldhistory.org/article/997/ancient-egyptian-agriculture/.

[22] Noura Anwar, "Aish Baladi: Bread of Ancient Egypt," *Arab America*, October 3, 2017, https://www.arabamerica.com/aish-baladi-bread-ancient-egypt/.

[23] Hala Barakat, "Giving Life: A History of Bread in Egypt," *Rawi Magazine*, accessed April 12, 2022, https://rawi-magazine.com/articles/bread-in-egypt/.

[24] Exodus 12:14-16

captives. They were the prerequisite for the Passover, the final act before the Divine deliverance of the Exodus. Later, unleavened bread sustained each new generation of Hebrew people and marked their most significant interactions with God.

Matzah, Hebrew for unleavened bread, is present at every major epoch in the redemptive story. For the first thirty days in the Wilderness, it sustained the Hebrews until God substituted it with manna from above.[25] Once they reach the Promised Land, the Hebrews replace manna with unleavened bread made from the first fruit of the grain there.[26] When they built the first dwelling for God, the Ark of the Covenant, he had them place the bread of the wilderness inside to represent his nearness.[27] And the ark was at the center of the Temple they built in Jerusalem.[28] During their exile from Israel and Judah, without the structures they had erected, the Passover feast with its Matzah was a reminder that God was with them wherever they were.[29] The presence of the unleavened bread at every turn reminds us that theology and faithfulness are not static, they are dynamic. They happen in real time. No matter where the Israelites found themselves, the bread simultaneously indicated a new beginning, and echoed something ancient. The ban on leaven during the commemoration of God's deliverance and the Hebrews' birth as an independent people signified that

[25] Exodus 16:4

[26] Exodus 16:35; Joshua 5: 11-12

[27] Exodus 16:32-34

[28] 1 Kings 8:1-6

[29] Doulos Hal, "The Feasts of Israel – Unleavened Bread," Bibleorg Blogs, December 24, 2020, https://blogs.bible.org/the-seven-feasts-of-israel-unleavened-bread/.

liberation was inextricably linked to an exodus from the tyranny and the logic of empire.

Bread without leaven contains only essential items; it isn't weighed down by extra ingredients. It has no additives, no preservatives, no added sweeteners.[30] It is just flour and water—flat and unpretentious.[31] Bread with leaven, like that of the Egyptians, became bloated as it rose and took longer to digest.[32]

The science of yeast—the most generic form of leaven—has powerful theological implications. Leaven alters, modifies, lightens, and distorts the distinctiveness, original flavor, and fragrance of dough. Too much of it diminishes the nourishment that comes from bread and makes it harmful. It creates holes that infiltrate the entire loaf, which becomes pale, ruptures, and collapses in the intense heat and pressure of an oven.[33]

In the New Testament, Jesus uses the concept of leaven to refer to the subtle and pervasive power and growth of the corruption of empires. First, he warns his disciples about the leaven of the Pharisees. The Pharisees were a sect of religious leadership within Judaism that promoted meticulous observance of the law and who were most popular amongst the common

[30] David Porush, "The Quantum Theology of Matzah: Science Delves the Spiritual Mysteries of Yeast," Telepathy, March 27, 2021, https://davidporush.com/2018/03/27/the-quantum-theology-of-matzah-science-delves-the-spiritual-mysteries-of-yeast/.

[31] Cookist, "Unleavened Bread: The Yeast-Free Bread Recipe Typical of the Jewish Tradition," Cookist.com, April 5, 2019, https://www.cookist.com/unleavened-bread-the-yeast-free-bread-recipe-typical-of-the-jewish-tradition/.

[32] THINK Magazine, "An Ancient History of Bread (Part One): The Child of Civilization," Think Magazine, October 20, 2021, https://thinkmagazine.mt/an-ancient-history-of-bread-part-one-the-child-of-civilization/.

[33] Michelle Michelle, "Too Much Yeast in Bread? What Happens & How to Fix It," BakingHow, August 31, 2022, https://bakinghow.com/too-much-yeast-in-bread/.

people at the time.[34] Jesus calls the infiltrating and harmful ingredient in their leadership hypocrisy.[35] He said the Pharisees made a habit of teaching righteousness but having no real intention to practice what they preached.[36] They said things and did not do them. They missed the forest for the trees by over-emphasizing the legal minutia of ceremonial righteousness and justice while ignoring the actual harm and exploitation taking place right in front of them. They tied up heavy religious burdens and laid them on people's shoulders and were unwilling to move them.[37] He criticized them for putting on pious, religious displays only so that people would notice them or so that they would sit in places of honor at banquets or synagogues.[38] Jesus scolded them for loving recognition and status more than God and their neighbors. As religious leaders, the Pharisees were supposed to demonstrate the love and nearness of God to the poor, but they distanced themselves from those they were meant to serve.

Jesus also warns of the leaven of King Herod and the leaven of the Sadducees. The leaven of King Herod has to do with arrogance and violence. Herod had the means and the prerogative to live without consequence. He used threats and intimidation to cut off the voice of truth-telling prophets, and actually had children slaughtered when he believed one prophecy meant that a young child would grow up to overthrow him.[39]

---

[34] Encyclopaedia Brittanica, ed., "Pharisee," *Encyclopædia Britannica*, August 20, 2020, https://www.britannica.com/topic/Pharisee.

[35] Luke 12:1

[36] Matthew 23:3

[37] Matthew 23:4

[38] Matthew 23:5

[39] Matthew 2:16-18; 14:1-8

The Sadducees were a sect of Judaism composed of high priests, aristocratic families, and merchants—the wealthier elements of the population.[40] They believed that authority came from social position and birth rather than strict adherence and piety like their rivals, the Pharisees.[41] The Sadducees sanctioned the actions of the oppressive Roman imperial leadership for the promise of prestige and power.[42]

Both the Pharisees and Sadducees are vocal in the gospels about their disdain for Jesus.[43] He refused to recognize the strict boundaries of the Law and the Tradition—both of which they regarded as essential to preserving the identity and moral superiority of Judaism.[44] They resented the freedom and liberality he took with the love and mercies of God to gentiles, women, and sinners.[45] Jesus warns the disciples that their posture toward him is a result of hidden realities. Their leaven of hypocrisy, egotism, violence, exploitation, and greed had coalesced in a form of Judaism that God didn't recognize or sanction.[46]

The Hebrews were meant to be an unleavened community, completely discordant with the social structure of the Egyptian empire. They were supposed to order their community around a commitment to demonstrate God's will for sustaining creation

[40] Encyclopedia Britannica, ed., "Sadducee," *Encyclopædia Britannica*, November 21, 2020, https://www.britannica.com/topic/Sadducee.

[41] Encyclopedia Brittanica, ed., "Pharisee," *Encyclopædia Britannica*, August 20, 2020, https://www.britannica.com/topic/Pharisee.

[42] Ibid.

[43] Luke 20:1-45

[44] Luke 11:37-53; Matthew 23:1-36

[45] Mark 2:7; John 4:27

[46] Matthew 23:30

and the wholeness of humanity.[47] The Hebrews followed a law code, called Torah, that emphasized decentralized political power and economic self-sufficiency for all in the community.[48] They were to build an inclusive table that removed the great disparities of wealth between the elite and the masses. Their experience of oppressive imperial domination was the source for their radically counter-cultural religious and political vision.[49] God's election of the Hebrews was a strategy to set them against the various empires and great powers of their time. From Egypt and Assyria down through Babylon, Persia, Greece, and Rome, they were meant to bear witness to a different way of life and stand in juxtaposition to the world around them as the nations rose and fell.[50]

A year into Donald Trump's presidency, I came to realize and understand why God told me to remember the bread of life. I was finally ready to be honest with myself about all the irregularities and holes I had ignored over the years since I'd met White Jesus. Whiteness was noxious yeast in the bread I'd received. It was having the exact same putrefying effects on my faith and worldview as Jesus said it would. Hypocrisy, arrogance, violence, exploitation, and greed had become the most consistent characteristics of my Christianity over time, and it was making me sick. Faith as I knew it had become

---

[47] Walter Brueggemann, *The Prophetic Imagination* (Philadelphia, PA: Fortress Press, 1978), 16-17.

[48] Millard C. Lind, "The Law and the Old Testament," in *Monotheism, Power, Justice: Collected Old Testament Essays* (Elkhardt, IN: Wipf & Stock Publishers, 2015), pp. 61-81.

[49] Walter Brueggemann, *The Prophetic Imagination* (Philadelphia, PA: Fortress Press, 1978), 16-17.

[50] Isaiah 49:6

flavorless and pale. There were rips and ruptures in my theology around life and death, heaven and hell, truth and mercy, and even justice and salvation. Worship songs I once enjoyed were now tainted and triggering. Discipleship wasn't a pilgrimage anymore; it was scripted and programmatic. Whiteness altered and modified the distinctiveness of a good God. It distorted my self-perception, my spiritual perspective, my sense of reality. And the pressure of my questions and lived experience collapsed the façade white evangelicalism had created around any real conversation about racism, injustice, or American history.

Whiteness is an ideology that normalizes the practices, beliefs, perspectives, and culture of white people so that they are the unspoken standard by which everything else is measured.[51] In other words, it is the normalizing of white supremacy. It was born of a foundational system of beliefs that regarded innocence, virtue, purity, authority, value, beauty, objectivity, and intellect as inherent possessions of white people.[52] Whiteness isn't an ethnicity. It is the subtext of everything whether theology, or ethics, or history, or economics. It is a logic and a hermeneutic—that is, a way to interpret and view the world. Like leaven, whiteness is the agent we cannot see that gives rise to many of the situations, institutions, and myths that we encounter every day.

In the Exodus story, God did not ask the Israelites to give up bread, just leaven. Unleavened bread symbolized the

[51] Cara Cancelmo and Jennifer Mueller, "Whiteness," Oxford Bibliographies, November 26, 2019, https://www.oxfordbibliographies.com/view/document/obo-9780199756384/obo-9780199756384-0231.xml.

[52] Gloria Wekker, *White Innocence:Paradoxes of Colonialism and Race* (Durham, NC: Duke University Press, 2016), 15-17. .

delineation between the people of Yahweh and the Empires all around them.

Jacob and his family went to Egypt in search of bread and ended up in bondage.[53] It was the same for me. My experience in white evangelicalism started with a spiritual hunger that the yeast of whiteness almost ruined over time. As I began recognizing and extracting the poisonous and putrid ideologies and belief systems that animated the Jesus I met there, I got free. Freedom happened for me the same as it did for the Hebrews: with a call to unleaven the bread of life.

[53] Exodus 1:6-14

I Met White Jesus in Hell

The back seat of my mother's 1986 Audi was furry. It had gray seats, and it smelled like Benson & Hedges Menthol 100's, copper pennies, and Estée Lauder perfume. I was 12, maybe 13, and I sat there picking at a hardened piece of watermelon Bubble Yum that either I or my brother stuck in the fur some time ago. My mom was listening to some preacher named Joyce Meyer on a cassette tape, crying, and talking to God. It bothered me.

"How do you even know that God is real?" I asked her from the back seat, unsure why I was so perturbed.

She smiled, wiped the tears from her right eye, turned to me, and said, "Why don't you ask God if God is real? He will always show you what is true, and you will feel it deep inside." She turned to put her eyes on the road again and suddenly gasped. "Oh my God!" she screamed while slamming on the breaks. An unsightly brown station wagon made a left turn at a red light and we stopped just before we T-boned it.

"Mom, look!" I yelled and pointed to a sticker on the passenger-side bumper of the wagon. Huge white blocked letters with gold outline read "GOD IS REAL." She started laughing. I was stunned. A tingling warmth made its way from the top of my head to my arms, and I took a breath. Then we *both* cried. "God is real," I thought to myself.

I already knew something was out there that could change a life. My mother's whole being and countenance were different since she'd been "born again." I was intrigued because I'd watched her try so many things to still her sadness, and this seemed to be the only thing that worked. Still, I didn't know whether God was interested at all in what went on down here on the earth. That was what I really meant by "real" when I asked my mother the question. Does God see and hear and care about me?

From that day on I started talking to God. I was a precocious kid and had a ton of questions for both him and my mother. Mom (dealing with a headache, I am sure) bought me a simple, unpretentious, black leather New Living Translation Bible with my name engraved on the front so I could read for myself. That Bible was precious to me. And even though it didn't answer as many questions as it provoked (my poor mother), I enjoyed reading it. I was fascinated by the way the words seemed to jump off the page and the stories it told. I didn't understand it but it felt good to read it. I plopped it open every day, like roulette, and read whatever page it opened to. There was something magical and mysterious and intriguing about this new spiritual awareness I had and I was hungry for more of it. I was falling deeply in love with this Jesus. The way he talked to people and described God was fascinating. When the wind blew, I felt like Jesus himself was speaking directly to me. I felt as though God liked hearing from me and spending time with me. But eventually my faith took a turn in a different direction, a wrong turn from which it took me more than two decades to recover.

When I was 17 years old, I attended what the friend who invited me called a "play." It was really a kind of simulation that took me on a walking path through graphic scenes of teen suicide, drug overdoses, premarital sex, rape, and drunk driving accidents. Then I watched as these wayward teens faced judgment and burned alive in the Lake of Fire from the book of Revelation. At the end of the experience, we stood in a room and waited. For what, I didn't know. My friend looked at me weird like she knew something I didn't.

"Wha—" Suddenly, before I could finish asking, a bright light appeared, and there he was: Jesus. He was standing at the top of a golden staircase with smoke all around him. This Jesus was different than the one in the pictures on the walls in my home—he was tall with straight brown hair and had thick eyebrows above his blue eyes. He smiled, showing his pristine white teeth and a small dimple at the corner of his chin, just visible below his manicured beard. He reminded me of an older version of Jordan Catalano from *My So-Called Life*. I felt a little embarrassed for thinking he was cute. I didn't know much about Jesus at that point, but I knew that was probably not an appropriate thought. This Jesus had a humongous book in front of him, and he kept looking down at it and back up at us. I guess he was trying to give the impression that he was searching. Maybe he was looking for a reason to let us leave? I wanted to get out of there. I was the only Black kid in the crowd. My parents' church never did *anything* like this.

I had just spied an exit when Jesus yelled, "YOU! YOUNG LADY, IS YOUR NAME IN THE BOOK OF LIFE?" I looked at my friend, mad because she didn't prepare me for the pop quiz. I also hoped she'd give me the answer, but she didn't. She just smirked. I shrugged. I felt that saying no would mean I had to stay, and I wanted out.

"I-own-know," I said, hoping my casual mispronunciation of *don't* and large shrug would hide my embarrassment, "you tell me." Jesus told me it was *my* choice and asked if I wanted my name to be in the book. Even though I didn't know why the book was important, I said yes.

Once the production was over the staff workers took me to a trailer and said we were going to go down the Romans Road. This turned out to be a guided tour through verses in the book of Romans which highlighted the theological doctrine they said I had to agree with if I wanted salvation.

The staff were keen on redefining and reframing my world. Since the near accident with the "GOD IS REAL" car, I'd always felt close to God, but they told me he was far away from me. They said my name couldn't be in the book until I repented of my sins and accepted Jesus. They said that though I had thought I was following God, I was really following something called my "flesh" the whole time. They told me God killed Jesus. What did Jesus even do to deserve that? I thought Jesus was a good guy. Why did God kill him? They told me it was because of me. They told me I had to identify as a sinner and admit that's who I was at my core. This was news to me.

My parents named me after themselves and my grandmothers. My father, Thomas, and my mother, whose middle name is Michelle, combined their names to make my first name, Tamice. And my middle name, Namae, is a combination of the middle names of my grandmothers: Leah *Naomi* and Dorothy *Mae*. Names are important to my family and testify to where I come from and who I am.

But after meeting White Jesus, I wasn't Tamice. I was a sinner. I wasn't distinct. I wasn't special. I wasn't anything really apart from sin. It confused me because White Jesus was adamant about my name on the golden stairs, and now I was finding out that he had no use for who I was as an individual.

The Romans Road was unpleasant, and I never wanted to travel it again. It made me feel bad about myself and bad for Jesus. Since the day my mom and I saw that bumper sticker, I had begun to love and inquire about God without knowing I owed him anything. What I was now learning felt overwhelming and heavy, like I'd been tricked. It seemed unfair. How could God be so mad at me for something I didn't know I was doing? What had I done in 17 years that was so bad to deserve the flames I saw in the play? The earrings I stole from the mall weren't even real gold, and now I had this divine target on my back! What if I had died before I met this Jesus? I'd said yes to the book without having any idea what I was getting into, but now I felt pressured by fear. When I arrived at the "play" I didn't know I was a sinner, I certainly didn't know I was going to hell, and I never in my years of inquiry felt as though God didn't like me. But by the time I left, I was convinced the Bible made all these things clear. But the burden of the new information seemed to dissipate once I said, verbatim, a prayer the staff gave me. After that, the leadership cheered and clapped and said there was a party happening in heaven for me. They encouraged me to bring two non-Christian friends to the play the next night. I filled out a big rectangular card that stated my name was in The Book, and I carried it in my pocket for the rest of the year as proof. I felt as if a weight had been lifted.

Granted, I had only just learned about the weight, but I was happy it was gone.

When I pulled up to my house, I jumped out and ran inside. I couldn't wait to tell my mom I was saved now and show her the card. I also showed her my new neon purple Extreme Teen Study Bible we had stopped to get on the way home. I could tell she was trying to be excited for me, but she couldn't hide that she was puzzled and pained.

"What happened to the Bible I got you?" I didn't understand why she cared so much.

Luckily, on the 15-minute drive from the Christian bookstore to my house, my friend's parents had prepared me for the fact that she might not be happy with my decision. They said I should think of any disagreement I encountered from here on out as righteous persecution because the world hates Jesus and would see that the person they hate now lived in my heart. I told my mom I had replaced her gift with a *real* Bible because I was a *real* Christian now. I repeated everything I could remember from the car ride and the play. The New Living Translation, though it was easy to read, was not accurate or trustworthy, and thus wasn't really "God's Word." I told her I needed to be careful who I listened to from now on and who I hung out with because Satan and some birds were going to come after me and take seeds from the soil, or something like that. I could see the pooling of tears in her eyes.

"Congratulations baby," she said. It took twenty years for me to truly understand why the tears she shed that night were not like the ones she'd cried in her Audi.

After the night in Hell, my Christianity developed in white evangelical spaces. I stopped going to church with my family.

Instead, I went with the friend who'd invited me to the play. I made sure to bring my rectangular card as proof in case anybody tried something funny or the Rapture happened. I saw White Jesus there every Sunday. He was the pastor. He wasn't dressed like he had been when we met on the golden stairs. They all dressed different there. Nobody wore stockings or cufflinks or hats or church shoes. White Jesus replaced his sandals, robe, and sash with Sperry loafers, pastel polo shirts, and khaki pants.

Their church was shorter than mine. The songs were boring, and people didn't shout "Amen!" I guessed it was because the pastor didn't ask them to, even though they always said "amen" at my parents' church whether somebody asked or not. Nobody told these people to talk to their neighbors or testify. Weirdest of all, they didn't have an organ, and they clapped on the one and three beats, instead of the two and four. I did appreciate the brevity of my friend's church service though because we could go to lunch afterward and I would still have the house to myself for a while before my parents' church was over.

I loved going to lunch because that's when I got to ask the leaders questions. The pastor (a.k.a. White Jesus) didn't remember me from the play, but I remembered him. He kept calling me Tynese. *Did he forget to write my name in that book? Did he write the wrong name?* I ignored those questions because everyone told me this man and the other pastors had all the answers.

They didn't talk as much about Jesus as I thought they might, but they did talk a lot about the Rapture and worldliness. They focused on how to be a good Christian, including dropping old, non-Christian friends, throwing away CDs of "secular" music, and never watching R-rated movies. When I asked about the differences I observed between my old church and theirs, they explained that they were more *serious* about their faith. They said maybe God had been calling me to their church so I could know him in a more meaningful way. I asked why God would send people to hell if God was all the things they said he was—loving, merciful, kind, and compassionate. They told me that I shouldn't question God, and the real question I should be asking was why any sinner would be allowed into heaven in the first place.

After a while they grew weary of my questions, which confused me. My goal was to learn as much as I could about Jesus. I wanted to be a good Christian. And God didn't seem to mind my questions before I was "saved." but they told me I had to show God respect by obeying him and not questioning him. Through time I came to learn that my questions had been the result of my insufficient faith. Now I was becoming the person God made me to be. I began to feel like most of who I was needed to die if I wanted to follow Jesus. They said that was correct.

Eventually, having answers and ignoring questions made me feel safe. I read voraciously. But anytime something didn't match up with my faith, I just asked a pastor, and they solved the issue immediately by telling me exactly what the Bible said. The Bible had *all* the answers to *all* life's problems, and I didn't need to look anywhere else. There was a thrill that came with possessing truth and having the Bible's divine authority to back it up. The certainty gave me confidence to evangelize. I started to feel a sort of spiritual invincibility. I was saved now, and it was my job to tell as many people that as possible, so that they too could be like me.

Buttered Rolls and Peppermints

Before I met White Jesus, everybody at my church was Black. My family went to a United Methodist Church in downtown Norfolk, Virginia. On the way there, we passed liquor stores and bodegas. We saw dilapidated buildings, abandoned shopping carts, and steam coming up from the sidewalks. The inside of the church was chilly, and the heater made a loud bang when it came on. The sanctuary had the smell of old carpet, wood wiped with Pine-Sol, and stale cologne. What I remember most was the lady who always sat in front of us (Black church has unofficial assigned seating). She wore enormous hats and always had lipstick on her teeth. She was nice, though, and every Sunday she would turn around and give my brother and me peppermints. They were the pastel kind that were smooth and buttery and sort of melted on your tongue. We laughed every time because she always had so many mints, but her breath was stinky. Church laugh is the best. Church *breath* is the worst.

While my brother and I argued over who was going to tap the lady and ask for more mints, Ms. Simmons was in the back making her famous yeast rolls. They were always hot when service let out. She would hand each family a block of rolls wrapped in aluminum. We were supposed to eat them at home, but they were so good that my dad would finish at least one while complaining about how long my mom was taking to talk to people in the parking lot.

Every week somebody would stand up and "give honor to God" for things like their niece finally coming home or their light bill getting paid. They'd ask for prayer for a grandson that "nobody can't seem to find," or for ailments like arthritis and gout. Then we sang. I loved when we sang.

Ima souuul-jah on the battlefield/ and I'm fightinnn/ yes, I am/ fightin for the Lord.

Everyone clapped or played a tambourine. All the syncopated rhythms made us sway and rock and bounce. The music would linger before the next song—"Thank yah Jesus!", "Hallelujah!", "Oh Glory! Glo-rrayy!" People would cry and wail. The people with the ailments and the testimonies shouted the loudest. If the shouting lasted long enough, the preacher cried out, "Y'all betta stop now, fore you get me to hollerin! He's been SO good!" But they'd just shout some more, even louder, and the organist would start the praise break. None of the musicians had sheet music, they just knew how to play together. It was effortless. It went on and on and on, but it wasn't boring. It was special. Service always ended after we took communion. This was my favorite part of church. We would sing a cappella songs about the blood of Jesus while we marched down to the altar to receive the elements.

When I fall on my knees/ with my face to the rising sun/ oh Lord, have mercy on me ...

At the cross, at the cross/ where I first saw the light/ and the burden of my heart rolled away/ it was there by faith I received my sight/ and now I am happy all the day.

The songs rolled into each other, one after the other, like the unfolding of collective souls into one. I felt things during those times that I still can't name. The feelings made me stare into the stained glass as the light broke through, and long to know the author of everything going on around me. It felt sacred and somber, and rich, and from here my love for communion grew.

Church was a staple of my upbringing, as it was in many Black families. But the church never talked about getting your name in the Big Book. It never put on productions that simulated suffering or hell. I suppose there was already more than enough suffering going on in the congregation's everyday life. Church was a refuge. That is probably why it always lasted so long.

But White Jesus taught me that my family's church had weak theology and couldn't "feed" me anymore.

The people at White Jesus' church were nice and generous, but I rarely saw anyone who looked like me, unless they were cleaning bathrooms or fixing lights. None of the families seemed to be struggling. They weren't living in homes like the ones I used to pass on the way to the church where I learned to love communion. It felt like a completely different world. They ate healthy foods and had "healthy" families that took bike rides and long walks. No one had gout. They bought organic produce, went on vacations, and had money for extracurricular activities. They sent out annual family photos, and hosted Bible studies and Christmas parties in their homes. White people just seemed to have a better, happier, and more exemplary life.

Even though I switched churches, Ms. Simmons and the lipstick lady always asked about me. They sent my family home with rolls and peppermints just in case I wanted some. My new church was so different—they still hadn't learned my name. Still, it felt like an upgrade. The carpet was cleaner, the building was nicer. They had a bookstore and a coffee shop inside the church. They didn't sing a cappella (they hardly raised their voices), but they had guitars, synths, a smoke machine, and stage lights.

I started to associate my parent's church with adjectives like emotional, dilapidated, and repetitive. I thought I was choosing my new church because it was better and more biblical. It was just a coincidence that all the serious Christians were white and all the books they gave me were by old white men named John. All of the leadership, all the conference speakers, all the musicians, all the "heroes," all the revivalists, all the theologians who "accurately" represented God just so happened to look the same. I thought I was maturing in my faith, but I was just leaving Blackness to become white.

My suburban upbringing gave me the skills to navigate White Jesus' church. I observed from a young age that there were two ways to be in the world. You couldn't talk about certain things at school the way you could talk about them at home with family. White people didn't mind if you were Black as long as you were not, you know … Blaaaaack. If you could take a joke and not be too sensitive, there would be no issues, and you could maintain the illustrious position of Black Friend.

My parents were HBCU graduates with master's degrees. They were part of the burgeoning Black middle class of the 1980s. We were one of a few Black families in our neighborhood.

My father worked in finance and my mother was a nurse. They never ceased to remind us that we were blessed to live where we lived, but that we needed to be respectfully careful of our words and actions. I think my parents lamented the need for us to learn these lessons, which is maybe why they looked so tired all the time.

Home life was different. In the house we were not to forget where we came from. We had Black art throughout our home. We attended Hampton University homecomings, tailgates, and football games. We went on a trip to see where Martin Luther King, Jr. was assassinated and made several attempts to celebrate Kwanzaa. We even went to see *The Wiz* on Broadway. I loved hearing my parents tell exciting stories about freedom fighters and P-funk.

They told sad stories, too. Stories about curfews during the riots in their neighborhoods after the assassinations of Dr. King and Bobby Kennedy. The story about police profiling while driving the New Jersey Turnpike in a car that was apparently too nice for a Black man to own. My dad worked hard for that car, but the officer still didn't think he deserved it. They made him lie on the ground on the side of the interstate while they searched it. Or the time another officer put a pistol to the back of my dad's head and said nobody would care if he pulled the trigger. Or my mom's stories about going to nursing school in the South, where professors doubted her intelligence and patients felt free to call her *n*gger*.

They showed us pictures of them in college with teased-out afros, holding KOOL 100's between the fingers of one hand and making Black power fists with the other. They looked happy, alive, and proud in those pictures, but they never looked like that when they left for or came home from work. Years of working in the white corporate world while protecting their Black children from stares and bias wore them down. My mom once shielded my two-year-old brother from a white woman who felt "unsafe" and refused to enter the locker room because my brother was in there and looking at her.

So, I knew what it took to navigate whiteness. But my new church taught me to worship it.

II
PART TWO

FAITH UNLEAVENED

Lessons from the Levees

The passion for Jesus I had in high school waned. I did not keep all those promises I made about staying faithful and pure at youth retreats. I hadn›t gone off to Bible College or joined Youth with a Mission like the truly faithful kids. I just went to college, and the youth pastor had said many times that's where faith goes to die. I'd even lost my Extreme Teen Bible and my Salvation card during an unfortunate canoeing incident. I figured I'd failed at Christianity. But during my second semester, after a near overdose, a possession with intent to distribute charge, a broken leg from beating my feet to go-go music at a night club, and a pending HIV test result, I decided that I should give the Jesus thing another try.

When I first arrived on campus, I got invited to a women's Bible study, but I was too ashamed of my backsliding to get involved. After my knee surgery, I decided I had nothing left to lose. I found the flyer they gave me and followed the directions, hobbling on my crutches. But it was a new semester, which meant I was in the wrong place. The leader of the men's Bible study for upper classmen meeting at the flyer's location that night saw my limited mobility and had compassion. They let me stay.

This Bible study was like nothing I'd ever experienced. The guys asked questions. They loved questions. And they were honest about being mad at God or even bored with him. One person even said cuss words and "Jesus" in the same sentence. I knew after that night I might like it there.

The guys invited me to a worship service the next night, and I went. There were so many people there, and I even knew some of the songs because I'd heard them at White Jesus' church. It could have been the warm spring walks in the evening to the group's events, or the fact that everybody seemed so happy and authentic, or the feelings I got when the lights dimmed and the worship leader strummed the E minor, but I appeared to be falling deeply in love with Jesus again.

The way we read and discussed scripture made Jesus seem so real, I was having "God moments" that were reminiscent of the day in the Audi with my mom. When the wind blew, I once again felt like Jesus was speaking to me. I thought that God liked hearing from me and spending time with me again. I was soaring. People in my chapter noticed and started to talk about "Tamice Passion." I talked to everyone about Jesus, and soon all my non-Christian friends started walking with Jesus too.

I quickly found myself in the group's leadership. Evangelism leader was the most undesirable position, second only to prayer team leader. It baffled me why no one wanted to talk to or about Jesus, but I offered to take both roles. I loved leadership, but over time, the relationships I had with people outside the Christian group changed. I became more of a recruiter than a friend.

My roommates my freshmen year were Black. They went to my high school and my parents' church, but I stopped hanging out with them completely. I never brought any of my new, white friends over to my apartment, and I never could quite figure out why. I felt embarrassed. I knew that much, but I didn't want to delve into which group of friends embarrassed me. I was hardly in the apartment, and when I was, I complained that they watched R-rated movies, cussed, and listened to secular music—all of which was a "stumbling block" to me and "grievous to God's spirit." They didn't like the Christian events as much as I did, and they told me I was changing. I told them that is what Christians do: we change. It's called sanctification, and it's a good thing. They begged to differ. By the time summer came, we went our separate ways, and I moved in with some girls from my small group.

But during my junior year, something happened that caused real friction between me and my new white, Christian friends.

"George Bush doesn't care about Black people."

That's what Kanye West said when he went off script during a televised celebrity fundraiser for the victims of Hurricane Katrina. I came home to my roommates watching replays on the news of Mike Myers' stunned face as he stood next to Kanye.

During my next small group, students from my fellowship argued about whether Kanye was right. Some people said it was uncalled for, though others conceded it was awful how long it was taking for aid to arrive to those poor Black people. I had learned to keep my mouth shut when we were discussing topics that had to do with race. I had had too many failed "race matters" conversations with them, and they had made their preference for colorblindness abundantly clear. But I was the lonely only in the group, and they looked at me to give the official response of Black people. I hadn't been paying close enough attention to current events, so I nodded along and pretended I agreed with both sides.

Fear of being unprepared again the next week drove me to stay up that night watching the news and doing research. I learned that a levee is a man-made mound of dirt or concrete designed to protect land from a flood.[54] Years of poor inspections and maintenance in New Orleans caused the levees to break, which is why the hurricane was so devastating.[55] Eighty percent of the city was submerged in flood water, and it didn't recede for weeks.[56]

The small group leader asked me to lead prayer at the next worship gathering. I hoped my newfound expertise on structural engineering would make the prayer more "anointed."

During my white evangelical journey I knew that, to be taken seriously, I could only share thoughts or opinions that came attached to a chapter and verse. I truly believed I shouldn't have opinions that didn't come directly from the Bible, even about a hurricane that occurred in 2005. So to prepare for prayer that week, I looked to the blogs of prominent faith leaders who my friends would recognize as knowledgeable and authoritative about the biblical take on current events.

One pastor said that sinners could not fathom that a loving God would have anything to do with a killer hurricane, but this

---

[54] Sacramento District, How Levees Fail & How We Fix Them, YouTube, 2011, https://youtu.be/A1IxIKLV68E.

[55] Peter Nicholson, "Hurricane Katrina: Why Did the Levees Fail?" Senate Testimony, November 2005, https://www.hsgac.senate.gov/imo/media/doc/TestimonyNicholson.pdf.

[56] Pruitt, Sarah. "How Levee Failures Made Hurricane Katrina a Bigger Disaster." History.com. A&E Television Networks, August 27, 2020. https://www.history.com/news/hurricane-katrina-levee-failures.

was because they were ignorant. He said that they were fools to think that God was their friend, when the Bible made it clear that God was actually their enemy, and the hurricane was proof that his wrath was on them. He quoted the same verses that I encountered the night I went down the Roman's Road. Another pastor wrote an article about God sending Katrina to punish New Orleans for gay pride parades. He quoted Romans too. All of the pastors I read decried the liberal media for making it about race.

I was confused about why Kanye blamed George W. Bush. But the blogs had an answer: Kanye wasn't bringing God into the equation. The blogs said "they" always make it about race when it isn't. Katrina was all "those people's" fault because "they" hated Jesus. Never mind that nobody was checking the levees near Black neighborhoods.

Their explanation was a hard pill to swallow. God was purposely letting grandmothers and aunties die from dehydration and heat stroke? God ordained this lack of access to medication and insulin? I remember looking at the tens of thousands of displaced people crowded in the Superdome on the news and wondering how it could be possible for anyone to hate God so much that they deserved to watch their loved ones drown or die of starvation. It made me want to cry, but I was afraid of speaking against God's Word and God's leaders. I "accidentally" overslept the day of the worship gathering, and showed up after the prayer time slot, just in time for communion.

Looking back, I can see that what I was really avoiding was what I call "those people theology." *Those people* theology sees inequity as a consequence of the collective misdeeds of a particular group or the individual bad choices of "others." It cloaks racial bias and ignorance in jargon about sin and depravity. It characterizes attempts to gather around a shared identity as separatism. And when called out, it claims reverse racism and persecution. *Those people* theology is responsible for the inability of my white evangelical peers to see the horror of systemic injustice or police brutality. It put Trayvon on trial for his own murder. The leaders at White Jesus' church preached this oppressive theology with hands lifted in worship and tears of longing for the Kingdom. I realize now the leaven in their theology kept them from true mourning, weeping, and lamentation. But whiteness had made me forget that *those* people were *my* people.

What I learned in my research on damaged levees turned out to be a perfect metaphor for the dissonance between the leaven of whiteness and *those people* theology on the one hand, and my own experience on the other. As I learned, there are a few major threats to a levee's stability.[57] Seepage occurs when water underneath the surface of a levee creates enough pressure to form a void in the structure, causing a section of it to collapse. When certain sections of the levee breach, it causes eventual devastation to the whole. Unlike seepage, erosion takes place on the surface of a levee. Over time, the accumulation of damage caused by the elements above ground depresses the levee, and it breaks. Finally, some levees are simply not big or sturdy enough to handle a large flood.[58]

My worldview was like a faulty levee. My theology couldn't withstand the power and pressure of my experience as a Black

---

[57] Ibid.

[58] Peter Nicholson, "Hurricane Katrina: Why Did the Levees Fail?" Senate Testimony, November 2005, https://www.hsgac.senate.gov/imo/media/doc/TestimonyNicholson.pdf.

woman in America. Theology is man-made. It's a construct humans develop to explain and understand the mystery of God and the way we should live given that knowledge. The unchecked whiteness infused into my theology eroded the goodness, substance, and safety of the gospel for me. It couldn't contain the flood of grief I felt watching young men and women die at the hands of those who were supposed to serve and protect them. The worldview I possessed was just no match for the world I inhabited. Black people were not safe, were not loved, and did not matter. Not to the President in 2005, and not now.

The day God told me to remember in that Atlanta church, I recalled the unease I felt when I thought that those families in New Orleans were recipients of God's wrath. For the first time, I began to retrace my steps and measure the distance my faithfulness to White Jesus had created between me and my Blackness. Ten years after Katrina, I felt unstable in my faith. I considered everything I'd ever learned a crock, and that started to make me feel like I myself was a joke. Then, in 2016, I learned that four out of five people I'd been with for small groups, mission's trips, evangelism, worship gatherings, and seminary classes voted for Donald Trump, a man who once called for the deaths of five Black teenagers for a crime they didn't commit.

Eighty one percent.

Almost the exact percentage of New Orleans that laid in ruins under the flood waters. My inattention to what was happening inside me as I persisted in white evangelicalism let the erosion of my faith happen. Whiteness destabilized my faith and caused the eventual collapse of everything I knew and believed.

Pendulums & Paradigms

Just before I left my college campus for summer break in 2004, someone handed me a copy of the album *Real Talk* by Christian hip hop artist Lecrae, and a book called *The Dangerous Duty of Delight* by John Piper. By the time I returned to school that fall, I'd finished two more of Piper's books, *Desiring God* and *The Pleasures of God*, as well as John Calvin's *Institutes* and Augustine's *Confessions*. In just one summer, I was proudly identifying as a "five-point" Calvinist, a particularly rigid wing of white, protestant theology in the US based (somewhat) on the teachings of Calvin, a French theologian. This way of thinking scratched the itch I felt for more certainty and a clearer understanding of God. Any questions I had or dissonance I still felt about God were due to the "total depravity" of my human soul. Any evil that happened in the world was somehow for God's glory. Anybody who wasn't following Jesus wasn't chosen. It was that simple. Everything happens according to a predetermined, divine screenplay in the mind of God, and that felt safe. Calvinism did not make God predictable, but it made him explicable. Even if I couldn't be sure what God would or would not do, I always knew why he did it, and that felt better than nothing.

My friends all felt the paradigm shift, but it did not comfort them. I was armed and ready with a plethora of obnoxious nuggets from my readings when dear friends came to me with their pain, problems, experiences, or doubts. I tried to excite them about the fact that God did not care about their happiness. It was not about them at all! They deserved hell, and the idea that a righteous God would give them breath was already more than they could ever have asked. I told them that God had predestined whether they would go to heaven before they were born, and they couldn't do anything good on their own even if they wanted to because they were spiritually depraved.

But my certainty by day did not match my inquiries at night. I hadn't changed who I was—the girl who had all those questions for her mom about God. I would lay my head on my pillow praying.

Why wouldn't you save everyone if you can? Are you not able to save everyone? What if someone wants you but you don't want them? How is it loving to eternally torment most people, especially if you preordained their waywardness?

They were legitimate questions, but by daytime I silenced them again, feeling guilty for my lack of faith.

Unsurprisingly, by that winter I was struggling to stick with Calvinism, though I would never have admitted it. My unanswered questions and self-hatred—the latter a byproduct of the frequent reminders about my depravity—were taking a toll. That's when I got ahold of the worship band Shane & Shane's new song *Yearn*. I listened to it relentlessly. It made me feel God's presence again; but since Calvinists frown upon feelings, I only listened in private.

One night a girl named Lauren heard me listening in my dorm and knocked on the door. She had the album too and invited me to a conference during Christmas break where Shane

& Shane would be performing. The conference, put on by a mostly white midwestern ministry, was all about God's love and affection for his people. At that point I had a tough time believing that God felt anything. On the slim chance that God felt *something*, it wasn't positive. and on the even slimmer chance that God felt something positive, it certainly wasn't aimed in *my* direction. I was wary of the topic and hadn't ever heard of this conference, but I was not about to miss an evening with Shane & Shane.

The first day was incredible. We arrived at 2:00 a.m., but we were too excited to go to our hotel, so we snuck into the auditorium and slept there. The conference kicked off with Chris Tomlin's brand-new jam *How Great is Our God.* There were at least 20,000 other kids my age in the stadium singing the words. It was majestic. I felt so many emotions during worship. I made tearful confessions, hugged people, uttered wholehearted commitments to God about being more disciplined, about prayer and quiet times, about being less lustful and more Christlike. I didn't know you could feel so much of God's presence at one time. My body felt electric and alive, my heart felt like it was soaring, and my voice was hoarse. The atmosphere was addictive, and I wanted to stay in that space and feel those things all the time.

During worship, the preachers and singers would interrupt the music by shouting phrases and sentences about how much Jesus liked me, delighted in me, had zeal for me, and would fight for me. *God is a lover, looking for a lover!* they sang. The music opened me up and the sentences poured into my heart. The boundaries that Calvinism erected were palpably expanding to make space for what they were calling the "bridal paradigm."

Jesus was not a stoic, distant king on a throne. He had a heart and felt passionate longing for his bride, the church. I hadn't ever thought of Jesus in a romantic way, but the invitation to think about Jesus as having feelings toward me like a fiancé was more than intriguing. I was overwhelmed.

As the music softened during worship that first night, a raspy voice began to speak:

> There's someone in this very room who knows it's time to give up that sinful relationship. There is someone here struggling with lust and masturbation, and same sex attraction. There is someone who's battling depression and suicidal thoughts. There's someone here in this room right now who is so ashamed that they've given up hope of relationship with Christ. There's someone here that has been asking God for more. They have been asking God to fill them. Beloved, if that is you, Jesus is calling you tonight. He sees you; he hears you and he wants to answer you. Others of you, Jesus is saying it is time to start over. To press delete on the past and sign up again. There are people standing at the front right now who are ready to pray with you, come forward and give it all to Jesus. Don't worry about your friends, this is between you and Jesus. Come now, Jesus is here. The Holy Spirit is here.

You could hear the sound of young people wailing and sobbing echo throughout the arena alongside the commotion of feet shuffling to prayer circles. The movement toward the altar started as a trickle but quickly became a flood. We all felt so seen by God. How could this random stranger know these things about us? Down at the front a sweaty hand touched my forehead, and my limbs turned to spaghetti as I suddenly felt lightheaded. When I came to, I was on my back with a black "modesty cloth" on top of me. All the other women had them too, but not the men. Feeling both embarrassed and energized, I peeled myself up off the floor, stepped over the stragglers on the ground, and returned to my seat. The preacher who started it all was gone. The lights had come up, and Bibles were opening everywhere. I had no idea how long I had been down there. But I realized quickly I should've stayed. The preaching was just as intense as the worship, and it too was followed by an altar call. I passed out a couple more times. This was only day one, and it felt like drinking from a fire hose.

All the sessions were equally passionate and evoked a sense of urgency. Everybody on the stage talked about Jesus in a way I'd never heard before, like they really knew him. I wanted that. They could hear his voice so clearly. On the way home I was determined to combine this type of faith with my own and become a charismatic Calvinist.

The result was fanaticism. Over the next three years on campus, I underwent a transformation. I began fasting three days a week. I only went to class for tests, spending most of my time holed up in my room listening to sermons and worship music, reading my Bible, journaling, and praying. Co-workers and other students in my dorm reprimanded me for playing my music too loudly, but I was doing it so others might come under the sway of Jesus. My friends and family complained that they never saw me anymore—that I never talked about anything except this conference, or issues the conference obsessed over like End Times prophecies. The passion that once made me the life of the party was now an obsession that made me a recluse. The ache to be back in my room worshipping swallowed up every moment I wasn't there. To do anything else or be anywhere else was unbearable. I was behaving like an addict. The need to satisfy my craving became overwhelming. The CDs weren't enough anymore; I had listened to them all too many times. I needed to *be* there at the conference again. Those were the only people who understood me. They wouldn't think my daily schedule was weird—they all had that schedule. In fact, their ability to maintain that schedule is what qualified them to be on staff. I chalked the concern of friends and family up to "the enemy's schemes," persecution for my righteousness, or their lack of seriousness about their faith.

At the same conference in 2007, a speaker shared a dream about Jesus appearing to her, striking her with lightning, and telling her that he made September 11 happen so that America would turn to him. Then a Black preacher who was a part of the ministry leadership took the stage and said that Jesus was calling Black people to join the ministry's movement. He shouted to us, "Now is the time! Now is the time! The Lord says to the Black community you are in Babylon with all your wealth and all your luxuries! Come out of her! Come out of Babylon says the Lord!"

It was the first time since meeting White Jesus that I saw a Black speaker on the main stage at a conference, let alone heard anything particular about being Black. The message and the atmosphere were too potent to garner a neutral response. It sealed my fate. The power of the preaching, the music, and the prayer had already made it impossible to enjoy my campus groups or church communities. Back home they just were not "on fire." They didn't care about the fact that Jesus was coming back. They didn't like to pray as often or fervently as they should. They didn't get me, and I didn't fit in there anymore.

Right there at the conference, I called my university and withdrew from school. After that, I called my parents and told them the news. They were in the middle of my grandfather's birthday dinner, and everyone there, understandably panicking, told me I was being drawn into a cult. But enough of White Jesus' followers had warned me about my family by that point. Family and friends only wanted my faith to be lukewarm because my devotion convicted them of their own tepid relationship with God. But I would not let them hinder my potential or sow doubt into the calling God had on my life.

I convinced my grandmother to buy me an early flight home from the conference so I could begin moving and start working for this ministry immediately. I got home, found someone to sublet my apartment, and packed everything I owned into my black 2002 Toyota Echo. I drove 18 hours in the middle of the winter from the Southeast to the Midwest and reported for duty at the ministry I had left less than three days before.

Missouri Compromise

I arrived at the mission's base in Missouri on my 24th birthday. I had full confidence in the ministry I was joining. Its origin story and reputation were enthralling. It started in a prayer meeting that began in the 1980s. One of the ministry's prayer and worship events had been going continuously for several years. I'm not joking. It was going around the clock, every day. No exception. People in charismatic circles knew the ministry as a place where God was moving. It had an atmosphere where Heaven was "open" and the "fire on the altar" never went out. People who joined saw themselves as "special friends" of Jesus who knew the secrets of his heart, like the disciples in his inner circle—Peter, James, and John. It was a bond we all shared. We were certain we would be messengers that prepared the way for the second coming of Christ, as John the Baptist did the first time around. The ministry trained us to help the rest of the Body of Christ (those not in our specific movement) understand Jesus correctly. Our "social justice activism" took the form of intercessory prayer. We really believed God moved at the sound of our voices in direct response to the consistency of our prayer and singing.

I was already acquainted with this ministry and with White Jesus so there was no culture shock. Of course, I was the lonely only in many meetings again, but I was used to that. And I was used to the particular kind of attention it brought me. If a new song came out that was not too secular and folks wanted to learn the dance, guess who got the floor. If they didn't understand some slang, I was their human Urban Dictionary. But these lessons were not about them wanting to learn parts of my culture. They wanted my legitimacy. They had a Black friend who taught them Black stuff. A Black friend who agreed with their beliefs and even worked for their ministry. So, the overwhelming number of white faces in their ministry was not, in fact, a sign of exclusion. Thank you very much.

Being Black in a white ministry in a red state hit different during the Obama years, though. I went from feeling exploited for my coveted cultural knowledge to feeling exhausted by it. And it wasn't just me. I didn't have many, but I had a few Black friends during that time. We found one another the way Black people do in white spaces. It starts with a double take, a nod that communicates *I get you and I got you*, and then that smirk that says, *I experienced a microaggression today*. If I had a dollar for the number of times a white person mistook me for one of the other three Black women with natural hair in the ministry, I would've had more than the $60 per month I was living off as an unpaid intern.

Not all the Black people were on the same page about what Blackness meant to them. For some of us, Blackness was an afterthought. For others, it was the token that granted access to power and position. Still others were trying to bridge the gap between these groups. It didn't matter though. We were in Missouri to answer the call we heard from the one Black speaker at that conference. We all felt the same ache and left everything behind to be there. We gathered despite our differences as often as we could and had conversations amongst ourselves that we couldn't have anywhere else. We laughed a lot, like when the worship leader used an 808 drum machine or played Fred Hammond and sheepishly glanced in our direction to see if we had noticed. We laughed when they asked one of us to do spoken word poetry in February, or when prayers for the Black community included phrases like "From the crack house to the White House, open up their eyes." Our times together were refreshing for all of us.

But in August 2008, when the Senator from Chicago accepted the nomination to pursue the presidency, we could no longer ignore the differences between our perspective and that of the wider ministry. Those differences were now a herd of elephants in the room.

When Barack Obama ran for President, it was such an exciting time for my family and for many people with skin like mine. My brother and sister-in-law stood in line outside for hours early in the morning so they could vote before classes started on their HBCU campus. My mom and dad texted me pictures with grins and stickers saying "Yes, We Can" and "I Voted." They even sent me a picture of my nephew holding hands with Obama at the Democratic National Convention.

Obama had swag. He walked just like my dad with a sort of bop in his step. His wife's complexion was the same as mine. Her attitude reminded me of my mother and my auntie. The Obamas made me feel proud, but I was too ashamed of that pride to tell anyone at the ministry. It would have made them question my devotion to Jesus. And out there, devotion was a really big deal.

Can We, Though?

The campaign was a somber time for us lonely onlys. There wasn't as much laughter, but I don't know if any of us could articulate why we were irritable. We were all at war within ourselves in one way or another. The white people kept reminding us that we were different by laying their hands on us unprompted and praying for "*your* community." The Black ministry leaders, who didn't seem to be at war within themselves at all, constantly exhorted us to show allegiance to Jesus above all else. They created an "alliance" for Black people in the ministry to "prepare the way of the Lord" in the Black community through prayer, truth telling, and bringing more Black people into the movement.

Most of the alliance meetings we had characterized Black leaders and churches outside our movement as overly emotional and lacking biblical depth. They warned us not to get swept up in movements for what they called "false justice" when it came to questions of race. They told us not to place Blackness before Christ. One meeting they spent two hours teaching about Martin Luther King, Jr.—how he was a false prophet that Black people had turned into an idol. With Obama, the Black community was committing idolatry once again. My familiarity with these notions and willingness to embrace them propelled me into leadership.

Many of my Black siblings walked out during this time. I should have, but I didn't think I could. I was so afraid of being wrong about God. I wanted Jesus to like me and trust me. I became the person who led the weekly prayer asking God to "remove the blinders from the eyes of the Black community" so they could vote for the "right" candidate. The ministry didn't need to worry about *me* backsliding. I was going to be faithful to Jesus even if it cost me all my friends and family, and it did. I wore the isolation like a badge of honor until it became a burden I could not carry any longer.

I was over a thousand miles away from my family at the time. When I tried to warn them about how dangerous Obama was for our country, they laughed it off. I was frustrated and confused. I couldn't celebrate with my family because I thought doing so would mean I didn't care about saving their wayward souls. Still, I was not entirely assimilated. Shunning the Obamas always put a lump in my throat. But just like White Jesus had discipled me to do, I tamped down my emotions and the questions that came with them. One alliance meeting, to prove my loyalty to the mission, I read aloud an email correspondence with my family, saying I "wanted feedback." I walked to the front, looked out at everyone, then down at my phone as I read the subject line: *To my friends and family, a heartfelt letter regarding the upcoming elections.*

In the email, I talked to my family about Planned Parenthood and the blood of innocent babies "crying out from the ground," about eugenics, and about America's impending judgment. I told them they were being deceived by the devil and needed to "come out of Babylon." I told them we were in danger as a nation if we elected Obama. I told them about

9/11 and the lady who felt the lightning. Obama would keep America under God's wrath because he supported gay people and women's rights. We couldn't vote for him. He wasn't fearful of Muslims like we were supposed to be; he might even be one of them. He wanted healthcare for lazy people who jerked the system. I warned them that they were putting their Blackness before Jesus and that they needed to choose what was right over their politics. I told them they would have blood on their hands if they chose sentimentality over the Spirit of God. It was quiet when I finished reading, and I had the sense that I'd transferred my uneasiness onto the whole group. I put my phone in my back pocket and started back to my seat.

I was just sitting down when someone turned and asked if anyone had responded.

I said, "My dad, and to be honest, I am not sure how to respond. Maybe y'all can help?" I read the response:

> Dear Meecie,
>
> Political choices are very personal ones, and this process is fairly new to you. You should examine all issues; single issue candidacies and philosophies have been far more destructive than you could imagine. Your choice is your choice, and no one should condemn you for it, you should however understand what the candidates are for as opposed to what they are against. Being against abortions doesn't mean much to someone who is disenfranchised and discriminated against.

It's your choice, just get all the facts. Remember people of your race and Senator Obama's have not had the opportunity for too long a time to exercise a vote. In fact, many died for that right and that too was ignored by many of those who use the single issue of abortion to diminish otherwise qualified candidates. We will never have a perfect candidate because we all want something different. We take our personal life experiences and history into the voting booth. As someone who has lived long enough to experience racism and Jim Crow laws, I clearly have my views.

Love,
Dad

Silence engulfed the room. Finally, someone spoke up. "God's Word is God's Word. It can't be bickered or argued with. You don't need to justify or explain it or prove yourself. You've spoken the Word of the Lord to your family, and not everyone has ears to hear or understand. They warned us persecution would happen, and it's happening."

At the end of the meeting, we prayed that we would remain strong, and that our enemies would not sway us.

And then he won.

Obama won!

White Sheets and Black Stories

We cannot see the air we breathe until something makes it visible to us. It is only by stepping out into the cold that we see what all is present to us and in us. Yet its visibility disappears as soon as we leave the cold and enter into a warm space. There, the breathing continues.

—Dr. Willie James Jennings[59]

When MSNBC announced that Barack Obama was going to be the 44th president of the United States, the leaders of the ministry called everyone into a Solemn Assembly. I didn't vote for Obama, but it felt wrong for people to be so sad about his victory. I sat down in the assembly and was pulling out my Bible when my cell phone rang. It was my grandmother. A wave of remorse and regret came over me.

Her name was Dr. Leah Naomi Omega Goldsborough Hasty. I called her Mom-Mom. She grew up in a segregated town on the eastern shore of Maryland. She was the second youngest of twelve siblings. They hunted their own food, and

---

[59] Willie James Jennings, "Supersessionism, Nations, and Race: Society for Post-Supersessionist Theology 2021 Annual Meeting," YouTube, December 9, 2021, https://www.youtube.com/watch?v=BDlFvKAGGTo.

they all shared one outhouse. Mom-Mom had seen so much, done so much, and this election victory must have felt like her experiences had not been in vain. But here I was in a quiet room of devastated white people mourning. I was grateful for the opportunity to step outside. Mom-Mom's call poked a hole in the suffocating silence surrounding me.

"Hello?" I answered the phone. I could hear people in the background cheering and crying.

"Hi ... Meecie?"

"Yes! Hi, Mom-Mom!"

"Are you watching the news?"

"No, Ma'am. I'm at a prayer meeting."

"A prayer meeting?"

"Yes."

It took a moment for her to reply.

"Oh, well, it's a momentous night, and I was just calling to celebrate and say I love you."

"I love you too, Mom-Mom. Thanks for calling. Tell everybody hi for me."

"I will. Take care of yourself."

"I will."

Click.

I headed back into the prayer room. The juxtaposition between my life before and after White Jesus was never more jarring than the moment I opened that door. The room was an echo chamber where white intransigence obstructed Black jubilation. My family was celebrating. My church was crying. I felt like an orphan.

As I sat back down, I pushed away the rumbling of roiling memories of stories my grandmother had told me that were threatening to erupt inside me and disrupt the noiseless gathering. I remembered her telling me that my great grandmother, Ida Jane, worked for a wealthy plantation owner as a laundress and maid. One day while ironing, she laid a white sheet out on the board and saw two holes. It was a Ku Klux Klan hood. The story goes that she folded the uniform up, put it in a drawer, and gave the missus her notice.

Then there was the time Mom-Mom took the train to hear Mary McLeod Bethune speak at a convention. She had complained that she looked ugly because of a scar that developed on her face after she fell onto a metal can. Ida Jane dragged Mom-Mom to the convention to show her that worth comes from the heart and mind, not outer beauty.

Mom-Mom marched for voting rights and participated in the sit-in that desegregated the ice cream shop in her neighborhood. She always said she did the latter because Ida Jane loved French vanilla.

I'm sure she carried these stories with her to the polls as she checked the ballot for a man with skin like hers.

White Jesus needed me to forget these stories. Myths like him can only function in the absence of reality. Story is too powerful. Notions, fabrications, and falsehoods cannot withstand the test of a testimony. White Jesus cannot endure the presence of people who need real-life liberation because his architect was the imaginations of the privileged. He needed me to downplay my inheritance because he could not stand up to it.

It was the last year of Obama's first term when Trayvon died. After his reelection, the 44th president went on national TV and said Trayvon could have been his son. I wondered if the president wasn't getting any sleep either. Had he noticed

Trayvon's shoes sticking out from under the blanket like me? The president may have been the only person who spoke to what I was feeling that day. The pastor sure as hell didn't. It broke me. That was the moment I finally let the lumps in my throat and the dissonance in my soul take the reins. The heat from my tears washed the scales out of my eyes. Someone— and certainly not just anyone—in a position of power had actually named my experience and validated the pain I was in.

There is hardly anything I regret more than missing out on the joy of Obama's election—such a crucial moment in the story Blackness is telling—because I was bowing to White Jesus. I can't help but feel a little like Ida Jane when I think about how Trayvon woke me up to the white supremacy in my theology. I'd stretched white evangelicalism all the way out over the years, and I, too, found holes.

I think my grandmother always knew that day would come. Mom-Mom died while I was in the middle of writing this very chapter. I find comfort and redemption in the fact that I drove her to the polls to elect the first Black, female Vice President of the United States. I held her storied hands while Kamala Harris was sworn in. A cancerous tumor had grown in on the jaw where the scar was. She was having trouble talking, but she managed a "go girl!" when Amanda Gorman let her literary light shine. She squeezed my hand when Michelle gave Kamala a fist bump on her way out of the arena, and I squeezed back. I'd finally come home.

When I told her I wanted to write this book one day, Mom-Mom winked at me. I'm winking back at her now.

Discomposure

White images and ideas dominate the reli-gious life of Christians and the intellectual life of theologians, reinforcing the "moral" right of white people to dominate people of color economically and politically. White su-premacy is so widespread that it becomes a "natural" way of viewing the world. We must ask therefore: Is racism so deeply embedded in Euro-American history and culture that it is impossible to do theology without being anti-black?

—James Cone[60]

"From the crack house to the White House, open their eyes." During a prayer meeting for the Black community, one of the singers in the ministry felt the "Holy Spirit" give her that line to sing. Worship leaders in the ministry came up with lines like this frequently. We called them "choruses" and we sang them over and over. We sang that chorus at least once a month during the Obama years. The ministry's headquarters was in

---

[60] James H. Cone, *Risks of Faith: The Emergence of a Black Theology of Liberation, 1968-1998* (Boston, Mass: Beacon Press, 2005), 131.

the middle of a Black neighborhood, but none of the residents ever came through. During a meeting, I mentioned that fact to a colleague on the leadership team, and he said, "Maybe we should serve fried chicken." When all the eyes looked in my direction to see how I would respond, I panicked. What do you say in a moment like that? If I get mad, then I can't take a joke. If I let it go, I'm a placating "Uncle Tom," and I'd have to bury my anger. These situations happened all the time, and I did what I always did: nothing. This is what made my exodus so excruciating. I'd stayed silent and betrayed myself a million times before I dumped White Jesus.

Until Trayvon, I never let myself sit and think long enough about the fact that my Black humanity had not been a part of the equation when it came to my relationship with Jesus. There were moments like Hurricane Katrina or the election, but for the most part so much of what I loved about being Black was left by the wayside in the name of "Christlikeness." I thought setting Blackness aside was a decision I had to make to prioritize my Christian identity. White people loved to talk about how ridiculous slavery was and how glad they were that we were past all that now. To them it was absurd to "get caught up" in a past which we could not change, and which had no bearing on the present. Our job was to focus on the Kingdom of God and strive toward Christian "unity," which was code for conformity.

Once I gave myself permission to question, my regret and remorse broke me. I was angry. I felt betrayed. I had given my *whole* life to White Jesus. My youth. My strength. My money. My time. My gifts. My tears. My talents. My fears. My desires. I had lent them all to the glory of this mythological savior. His cause had become my own. And for what? White Jesus didn't give a shit about me or anyone like me, and it wasn't even my choice that I was Black. God made me Black, and that was a liability in the society that he in his supposed sovereignty set me in. It didn't make sense.

The discomposure caused physical pain. I wanted nothing to do with White Jesus anymore, but he was everywhere— the books, the sermons, the music. They had even turned him into a bobblehead! Reminders of him now caused me to break out in hives, as if my whole body was revolting against the idea. I didn't want White Jesus anymore, not as a savior, king, a husband or a homeboy. I didn't care about going to hell for having the "wrong" theology anymore. I needed theology that would get me out of bed in the morning.

FAITH UNLEAVENED

III
PART THREE

White Jesus: An Origin Story

We ought not therefore to have anything in common with the Jews, for the Savior has shown us another way ... and consequently, in unanimously adopting this mode, we desire, dearest brethren, to separate ourselves from the detestable company of the Jews. ... How can they be in the right, they who, after the death of the Saviour, have no longer been led by reason but by wild violence, as their delusion may urge them? ... it would still be your duty not to tarnish your soul by communications with such wicked people [the Jews]. ... it is our duty not to have anything in common with the murderers of our Lord.

—Emperor Constantine at
the Council of Nicaea, 325 AD[61]

It's the fourth century.

The original followers of Jesus and their protégées have died. Rome's destruction of the Temple has created a diaspora

---

[61] Eusebius, Philip Schaff: NPNF2-14. *The Seven Ecumenical Councils* - Christian Classics Ethereal Library, accessed November 7, 2022, https://www.ccel.org/ccel/schaff/npnf214.vii.x.html.

of Jews from Jerusalem.[62] Emperors Galerius and Diocletian are persecuting huge numbers of Christians,[63] and the canonization of the Bible is close to finalization.[64] For the last three centuries, churches have flourished despite many significant variations in doctrine.[65] No one knew how suddenly all of this was about to change.

In the year 312 CE, the pagan emperor Constantine defeated his brother Maxentius at Milvian Bridge to complete his campaign to consolidate power and become the next Emperor of Rome.[66] The night before the battle, he allegedly had a vision where a voice told him to have his soldiers fight under the banner of Jesus Christ,[67] associating Jesus with military victory for the first time in history.[68] The next day, his troops won the battle at Milvian Bridge, and Constantine interpreted these events as a sign that the Christian God supports his imperial efforts.[69] He ordered his men to continue to fight carrying a symbol of Jesus, and they saw many more military victories. In the wake

---

[62] Kate Lohnes, "Siege of Jerusalem," *Encyclopædia Britannica*, August 29, 2018, https://www.britannica.com/event/Siege-of-Jerusalem-70.

[63] Arthur James Mason, *The Persecution of Diocletian a Historical Essay* (Cambridge: Deighton, Bell, 1876), 189.

[64] Anne Yarbrough, "Christianization in the Fourth Century: The Example of Roman Women: Church History," Cambridge Core (Cambridge University Press, July 28, 2009), https://www.cambridge.org/core/journals/church-history/article/abs/christianization-in-the-fourth-century-the-example-of-roman-women/5B483E0AAFA9D0C-BA8AD282BD488530F.

[65] Bart D. Ehrman, "Early Christianity: Diversity and Disparity," Wondrium Daily, June 13, 2022, https://www.wondriumdaily.com/early-christianity-diversity-and-disparity/.

[66] "Battle of Milvian Bridge." *Encyclopædia Britannica*, Accessed December 8, 2022. https://www.britannica.com/topic/Battle-of-the-Milvian-Bridge.

[67] Eusebius, *Life of Constantine* (Kingston upon Thames, UK: Limovia.net, 2013).

[68] Latourette, Kenneth Scott. In *A History of Christianity: Volume 1 /Beginning to AD 1500.*, 242–43. New York: Harper & Row, 1975.

[69] Ibid.

of these conquests, Constantine used a pagan version of Christ as a divine source of authority.[70] The next year, Constantine proclaimed a new law, the Edict of Milan, which put an end to the persecution of Christians. He invited church leaders to sit at the table of political power alongside him, and most of them did.[71]

He had the first Christian empire. But elevating Christianity to a place of power put increased pressure and importance on a vast array of theological differences among Christian leaders.[72] Those differences became not just disagreements, but fierce, destabilizing political battles. For instance, Athanasius, Bishop of Alexandria, and a key figure in the establishment of the biblical canon, was in the throes of an ugly debate with a man named Arius. Whereas Athanasius taught that Jesus is eternal and begotten of the Father, Arius was telling people that there must have been a moment in time when Jesus didn't exist.[73] The debate became so heated that it threatened to split the Church and, therefore, the new Christian empire.[74]

[70] Lawlor H. J., Eusebius, and Oulton John Ernest Leonard, *The Ecclesiastical History: In Two Volumes: Volume II* (London, UK: Cambridge, Mass, 1964), 367.

[71] Kimberley Fowler, "Eusebius of Caesarea, Life of Constantine I.26, 28-29," Eusebius of Caesarea, Life of Constantine I.26, 28-29, June 26, 2018, https://www.judaism-and-rome.org/eusebius-caesarea-life-constantine-i26-28-29.

[72] Paul A. Crow and et.al., "The Alliance between Church and Empire," *Encyclopædia Britannica*, 2019, https://www.britannica.com/topic/Christianity/The-alliance-between-church-and-empire.

[73] Andy Witchger, "Arianism, Athanasius, and the Effect on Trinitarian Thought," DigitalCommons@CSB/SJU, May 2005, https://digitalcommons.csbsju.edu/sot_papers/24/.

[74] Thomas G. Elliot, "The Language of Constantine's Propaganda ," The American Philological Association (JSTOR, 1990), https://www.jstor.org/stable/283996, 349-353.

To settle the matter, Constantine called together the Council of Nicaea in 325 CE.[75] His interference was political, and his strategy was simple: establish universal imperial doctrine so that rejection of any official Christian belief was also a rejection of the empire.[76] The resulting Nicaean Creed became a pledge of allegiance to Rome's redefinition of a Jewish faith.[77]

Constantine blamed the Jews for the death of Jesus[78] and at the Council of Nicaea, called upon the 300 Bishops that had gathered to reject and have nothing in common with them. He called the Jewish people detestable and accursed, removed the Hebrew calendar as a reference for Christian tradition,[79] and nothing in the Creed mentioned the Jewishness of Jesus.[80]

The Creed changed everything.

Constantine's conversion and antisemitism transitioned the Church from a diverse, eclectic, and persecuted minority to a powerful, hegemonic, imperially-supported majority.[81] Western Christianity, under the control of the Bishop of Rome,

---

[75] Eusebius, Philip Schaff: NPNF2-14. The Seven Ecumenical Councils - Christian Classics Ethereal Library, accessed November 7, 2022, https://www.ccel.org/ccel/schaff/npnf214.vii.x.html.

[76] A. Edward Siecienski, *Constantine: Religious Faith and Imperial Policy* (England, UK: Routledge, 2017).

[77] Robert M. Grant, "Religion and Politics at the Council at Nicaea: The Journal of Religion: Vol 55, No 1," The Journal of Religion, January 1, 1975, https://www.journals.uchicago.edu/doi/abs/10.1086/486406.

[78] Eusebius, *Life of Constantine* (Kingston upon Thames, UK: Limovia.net, 2013), Vol. III Ch. XVIII.

[79] Ibid.

[80] Bernard Lazare, *Antisemitism, Its History and Causes* (21 Duane St, NY: International Library Publishing Company, 1903), 67; Ervin Budiselić, "The Importance of the Jewishness of Jesus for Interpreting the Gospels," *Edinost in Dialog* 76, no. 1 (2021): pp. 47-48, https://doi.org/10.34291/edinost/76/budiselic.

[81] Margaret M Mitchell, Frances M Young, and K. Scott Bowie, eds., *The Cambridge History of Christianity: Volume 1: Origins to Constantine* (Cambridge: Cambridge University Press, 2006), 573.

became the dominant form of the faith. As the fourth century turned into the fifth and sixth, the wealth of the Empire built ornate cathedrals and funded iconography that visually depicted Jesus for the first time. Believing in the superiority of European features, artists rendered Jesus as a European man.[82] Consequently, Jesus *became* one of the people who would eventually deem themselves the master race, white.

But he wasn't born that way.

White Jesus is the culmination of several decisive moments in Church history, the most important of which was the disconnection of Jesus the Nazarene from his Jewish life, history, and flesh. An abstracted, landless Jesus can shape shift. That Jesus will look for new flesh that can affirm and demonstrate its values. Those values were the supremacy of doctrine, creating enemies out of "others," and obtaining power and political control through violence. It found those values in a new, European body. Jesus became a symbol who lived in the heart and mind rather than a man who lived in Roman-occupied Palestine.

Whiteness and White Jesus are the instruments of European conquest and colonization. Missionaries and settlers brought with them a Western imperial theology severed from the beauty, the particularity, the meaning, and the rootedness of the Jewish identity and religion of Jesus.[83] Protestant colonialists believed in their "Manifest Destiny." They saw themselves, not the Jews, at the center of God's salvific purposes and they

---

[82] The Root, ed., "How Jesus Became Widely Accepted as Being White: Unpack That," YouTube, December 13, 2018, https://youtu.be/dfJCyDmTwyg.

[83] J. Kameron Carter, *Race a Theological Account* (Oxford: Oxford University Press, 2008), 6-7.

replicated the imperial impulse to govern, exploit, and extermi-
nate in the Americas.[84]

There is no context to White Jesus.

There is no social location to White Jesus.

White Jesus cannot claim a place, a people, or a culture because White Jesus isn't rooted anywhere. He's imaginary. He's a
symbol that people in power co-opt to suit their purposes. To
them he is nothing and everything at the same time. He can be
a crusader, a soldier, a capitalist, a patriot, a colonizer. He can
be a White, American, middle-class man.

To become like this Jesus means becoming less like the people to whom he is contrasted —Jewish, Black, feminine, poor,
immigrant, or any number of other people. *This is White Jesus'
sanctification.*[85] This is his leaven.

---

[84] Conrad Cherry, *God's New Israel: Religious Interpretations of American Destiny*
(Chapel Hill, NC: University of North Carolina Press, 1998), 116.

[85] Alexander Jun et al., *White Jesus the Architecture of Racism in Religion and Education*
(New York, NY: Peter Lang, 2018).

Sidewalks

Trayvon's death and the aftermath sent me on a quest to understand how anyone could believe that a Black teenager minding their own business could be so dangerous. George Zimmerman said he shot Trayvon in self-defense.[86] The defense hauled a slab of concrete into the courtroom as an exhibit to assert that both men were armed with deadly weapons: Zimmerman had a 9mm handgun and Trayvon had the sidewalk.[87] Apparently, when Trayvon tackled Zimmerman, he'd broken his nose.[88] They showed the jury pictures of the defendant's swollen nose as corroboration. The jury declared Zimmerman was not guilty.[89] He succeeded in his self-defense argument. My fellow church members and ministry colleagues were adamant that the whole thing was unfortunate, but "the law was the law." Trayvon was just in the wrong place at the wrong time—a phrase that perpetually haunts people with skin like mine. It kept me up at

[86] Douglas O. Linder, "The George Zimmerman Trial: An Account," The George Zimmerman trial: An account, accessed 2022, http://law2.umkc.edu/faculty/projects/ftrials/zimmerman1/zimmermanaccount.html.

[87] NBC News, ed., "Attorney Uses Cement Prop in Zimmerman Trial," NBCNews.com, September 15, 2022, https://www.nbcnews.com/video/attorney-uses-cement-prop-in-zimmerman-trial-37003331579.

[88] Douglas O. Linder, "The George Zimmerman Trial: An Account," The George Zimmerman trial: An account, accessed 2022, http://law2.umkc.edu/faculty/projects/ftrials/zimmerman1/zimmermanaccount.html.

[89] Ibid.

night: how could the murder of this 17-year-old boy provoke no accountability of any kind? I needed answers, so I went looking. That quest led to a deep dive into American history.

Congress passed laws in the 18th century that designated free white persons as the only class of people that had the right to become citizens and own land.[90] Whiteness was therefore more than a racial identity; it was property. It held a particular value, giving its owner equity in society. The law protected that value by punishing anyone who didn't possess white skin. Only white people had the guarantee of the presumption of innocence in criminal matters[91] and of never being enslaved.[92] The "American Dream" was directly connected to one's possession of and proximity to whiteness.[93]

The legal classification of whiteness came with goodies both visible and invisible, like wealth, land, upward mobility, the benefit of the doubt, and civil liberties. But European settlers also saw themselves as the chosen, the elect who were commissioned by God and the Bible to build a shining city on a hill.[94] The cultural bond between Western European values

---

[90] University of Texas, ed., "Nationality Act of 1790," Immigration History, January 31, 2020, https://immigrationhistory.org/item/1790-nationality-act/.

[91] Lisa Marie Cacho, "The Presumption of White Innocence," *American Quarterly* 66, no. 4 (2014): pp. 1085-1090, https://doi.org/10.1353/aq.2014.0078.

[92] William Walter Henning, ed., "Slavery and the Making of America . the Slave Experience: Legal Rights & Gov't: PBS," Slavery and the Making of America . The Slave Experience: Legal Rights & Gov't, PBS, accessed November 7, 2022, https://www.thirteen.org/wnet/slavery/experience/legal/docs1.html.

[93] Ayan Abdulle and Anne Nelun Obeyesekere, "An Exploratory Paper on Understanding Whiteness," in *New Framings on Anti-Racism and Resistance. Volume 1. Anti-Racism and Transgressive Pedagogies* (Dordrecht: Sense Publishers, 2017), pp. 23-24.

[94] Katharine Gerbner, *Christian Slavery Conversion and Race in the Protestant Atlantic World* (Philadelphia, Pa, PA: University of Pennsylvania Press, 2018).

and Christian beliefs was so strong they became synonymous.[95] Protestant colonialists saw a correlation between nonwhite peoples and savagery, and an inverse correlation between intellect and melanin.[96] They also spiritualized salvation to pertain to the soul and not the body, which meant that their brutality always had the "silver lining" that they were Christianizing and saving their victims.[97] Just as it had been on the other side of the ocean, being Jewish or being non-white—being other—was concretely political in the Americas.

What happened to Trayvon that night didn't happen in a vacuum, it wasn't an isolated incident. There were layers of history and dehumanization beneath the actions, biases, and impulses of the man who took his life, those of the men who killed the people who followed, and those of everyone who excused them.

Stephon Clark was shot eight times in his grandmother's backyard just two years after Philando Castile was killed.[98] The officers involved were not prosecuted because, like in the case of Rekia Boyd,[99] they said they thought the cell phone he was holding was a gun. And though Clark had his back to them, they

[95] S Yvonne C. Zimmerman, "Cultural Foundations of Moral Imagination," *Other Dreams of Freedom*, 2012, pp. 103-129, https://doi.org/10.1093/acprof:oso/9780199942190.003.0005.

[96] CalvinJohn Smiley and David Fakunle, "From 'Brute' to 'Thug:' the Demonization and Criminalization of Unarmed Black Male Victims in America," *Journal of Human Behavior in the Social Environment* 26, no. 3-4 (2016): pp. 350-366, https://doi.org/10.1080/10911359.2015.1129256.

[97] Ibid.

[98] Frances Robles and Jose A. Del, "Stephon Clark Was Shot 8 Times Primarily in His Back, Family-Ordered Autopsy Finds," *The New York Times*, March 30, 2018, https://www.nytimes.com/2018/03/30/us/stephon-clark-independent-autopsy.html.

[99] Samuel Momodu, "Rekia Boyd (1989-2012) ," Rekia Boyd, March 22, 2021, https://www.blackpast.org/african-american-history/boyd-rekia-1989-2012/.

feared for their lives. That same year on the 6th of September, in Dallas, Texas, Amber Guyger shot and killed Botham Jean. Believing she was in her own apartment, she thought he was an intruder and opened fire.[100] The bullet traveled downward through the chest, hit a rib, and struck Botham's heart. He died sitting on his couch eating a bowl of ice cream.[101] In Fort Worth, Texas the next year during the early morning of October 12, Atatiana Jefferson was at home. She was playing video games with her nephew, and, like Botham,[102] she had a faulty front door lock which sometimes left the door open. Seeing the door cracked open, a neighbor called the non-emergency number to request a welfare check.[103] Upon arrival, Officer Aaron Dean saw Atatiana in the window and opened fire. She bled to death in front of her 8-year-old nephew.[104]

While Elijah McClain was walking home from the gas station like Michael Brown was, and listening to music the same as Jordan Davis, some passersby spotted him.[105] He was moving his arms to the music, which was in his headphones.

---

[100] Anne Branigin, "Medical Examiner Testifies Botham Jean Was Likely Bent over or on His Back When Amber Guyger Shot Him," *The Root*, September 26, 2019, https://www.theroot.com/medical-examiner-testifies-botham-jean-was-likely-bent-1838498730.

[101] Li Cohen, "Amber Guyger Asks to Be Acquitted Murder Charge in Death of Botham Jean," CBS News (CBS Interactive, August 8, 2020), https://www.cbsnews.com/news/amber-guyger-trial-former-cop-appeals-murder-charge-in-death-of-botham-jean/.

[102] Author: Tasha Tsiaperas, "Botham Jean's Apartment Door Was Unlocked When Dallas Officer Walked in, Shot Him," wfaa.com, September 24, 2019, https://www.wfaa.com/article/news/special-reports/botham-jean/botham-jeans-apartment-door-defective-unlocked-when-dallas-cop-walked-in/287-1019ecde-7b57-4eca-9568-8322c4a72c3d.

[103] "Atatiana Jefferson." Say Their Names - *Spotlight* at Stanford, August 6, 2020. https://exhibits.stanford.edu/saytheirnames/feature/atatiana-jefferson..

[104] Ibid.

[105] Lucy Tompkins, "Here's What You Need to Know About Elijah McClain's Death," *New York Times*, January 18, 2022, https://www.nytimes.com/article/who-was-elijah-mc-clain.html.

The motion made the onlookers nervous that he might be "sketchy," the same word used to describe Tamir Rice and John Crawford in the 911 calls that made their names hashtags. Elijah was anemic and got cold easily, so even though it was August, he was wearing a ski mask on the day he died.[106] Three police officers approached the unsuspecting 23-year-old autistic massage therapist and held him on the ground for 15 minutes in positions eerily similar to those in which the cops held Alton Sterling.[107] Elijah's arms were handcuffed behind him like Freddie Gray's,[108] but still, one of the officers applied a carotid control hold like the one that killed Eric Garner.[109] That stopped the blood flow to Elijah's brain, and Elijah passed out. When he came to, he told the officers he couldn't breathe, again like Garner.[110] He told them he had his ID, which is what Philando told the officer the day his little girl watched him die.[111] He said his name, something the hashtags for Sandra Bland taught us all to do. He told them where he lived, and who he was, but it didn't matter.

"My name is Elijah McClain," he said. "That's my house. I was just going home."

[106] *The Denver Post*, ed., "Elijah McClain Timeline: What Happened That Night and What Has Happened Since," *Denver Post*, June 26, 2020, https://www.denverpost.com/2020/06/26/elijah-mcclain-timeline-aurora-police/.

[107] Catherine E. Shoichet, Joshua Berlinger, and Steve Almasy, "Alton Sterling Shooting: Second Video of Deadly Encounter Emerges," CNN, July 7, 2016, https://www.cnn.com/2016/07/06/us/baton-rouge-shooting-alton-sterling/index.html.

[108] BBC News, ed., "Freddie Gray's Death in Police Custody - What We Know," BBC News, May 23, 2016, https://www.bbc.com/news/world-us-canada-32400497.

[109] "Chokehold: The Record," The Marshall Project, October 31, 2022, https://www.themarshallproject.org/records/825-chokehold.

[110] Ibid.

[111] German Lopez, "Philando Castile Minnesota Police Shooting: Officer Cleared of Manslaughter Charge," Vox, July 7, 2016, https://www.vox.com/2016/7/7/12116288/minnesota-police-shooting-philando-castile-falcon-heights-video.

He tried to tell them he was an introvert.

"I'm just different. That's all. I'm so sorry. I have no gun. I don't do that stuff. I don't do any fighting." It didn't matter. "Why are you attacking me? I don't even kill flies! I don't even eat meat!"[112]

Elijah McClain was only five feet six inches tall and weighed just 140 pounds.[113] But his words weighed on all of us much more than that.

Then came Ahmaud Arbery.

He was jogging through a white suburb.

The men who killed him were indignant that he would not stop, listen, and obey them, although they displayed no visible sign of their authority over him other than being white and male.[114] He was trespassing just by being. It took more than two months for the men to be arrested, along with the neighbor who filmed the lynching.[115] They would not have been arrested at all because two of the men were friends with law enforcement officials, and Georgia had an 1860s citizen's arrest law in place which made their story about trespassing a feasible defense. They wouldn't have been arrested at all had it not been for one of their own lawyer's miscalculated decision to

---

[112] "Body Worn Camera Regarding the in-Custody Death of Elijah Mcclain," YouTube, November 22, 2019, https://youtu.be/q5NcyePEOJ8.

[113] Lucy Tompkins, "Here's What You Need to Know About Elijah McClain's Death," *New York Times*, January 18, 2022, https://www.nytimes.com/article/who-was-elijah-mc-clain.html.

[114] Richard Fausset, "What We Know about the Shooting Death of Ahmaud Arbery," *New York Times*, April 28, 2020, https://www.nytimes.com/article/ahmaud-arbery-shoot-ing-georgia.html.

[115] Char Adams, "'They Almost Got Away with It': How a Leaked Video Led to Convictions in the Ahmaud Arbery Case," NBCNews.com (NBCUniversal News Group, November 24, 2021), https://www.nbcnews.com/news/nbcblk/-almost-got-away-leaked-video-led-convictions-ahmaud-arbery-case-rcna6690.

release the cell phone video.[116] They hunted and killed Ahmaud in broad daylight because they were just as confident of their place in the system as all the other perpetrators.

The killers equated their victims with danger and evil even when their backs were turned. The people on the never-ending list were killed by men who thought they didn't belong. They were killed because they didn't pass some subconscious test or obey the unspoken rule of knowing their place. Being Black is not safe in America. We run the risk of death just for having the audacity to take up space.

---

[116] Ibid.

Stolen Election

*Resist imperial hegemony and you bring to
the surface what is, inevitably, always part of
empire: domination based on violence. As it
was in Jesus' day, so it remains today.*

—Nathan Yoder[117]

"Oh my god' y'all see what they doin?"

"Turn on the news!"

On January 6, 2021 my Black friend group chats were
blowing up.

"Y'all see these white folks?"

"I hate it here."

"They really trying to take over the government rn."

"Smh."

I turned on the news, and the scenes were surreal. A mob
of white people storming the Nation's Capital, climbing buildings, and attempting to hold the government hostage to hate
and bigotry. There was not a mask in sight—neither to hide
the faces of the insurrectionists nor to protect anyone from
the COVID-19 virus. I turned the TV off and felt my heart

[117] Ted Grimsrud, *Exiles in the Empire: Believers Church Perspectives on Politics:
Papers Presented at the Fifteenth Believers Church Conference, September 2004*, ed.
Nathan E. Yoder and Carol A. Scheppard (Kitchener, Ont.: Pandora Press, 2006), 38.

pounding. I couldn't get the pictures out of my mind. Those people were armed and dangerous. They were calling our nation's representatives by name in tones reminiscent of Jack Nicholson in *The Shining*.

Just six months earlier, a week after the murder of George Floyd, Metropolitan police officers in Washington DC wearing riot gear and riding horses disbursed peaceful Black Lives Matter protestors around Lafayette Park with tear gas.[118] They cleared the way for Donald Trump to walk to St. John's Episcopal Church and pose for a now-infamous photo op holding a Bible. The difference in the treatment of these two groups of protestors came from the same principality of whiteness.

By January 2021, I was actively and publicly washing my hands of the leaven, so I took to Facebook to state my abhorrence.

"Whiteness is Terrorism. Turn on the TV and watch it work." Not too long after I posted, a friend responded to me in the comments.

"This is how America gets made great! Go Jesus! Stop the Steal!" I knew this person well. We'd done several missions trips together. And I couldn't believe the audacity and callousness.

She was excited about overturning a legitimate election, and all I could think about was Laquan McDonald, or Sean Bell, or Amadou Diallo, or any number of other Black people whose bodies were filled with holes after a police encounter. Only 52 people were arrested on January 6, compared to the 427 arrests of people peacefully protesting George Floyd's death between

---

[118] Tom Gjelten, "Peaceful Protesters Tear-Gassed to Clear Way for Trump Church Photo-Op," NPR, June 2, 2020, https://www.npr.org/2020/06/01/867532070/trumps-un-announced-church-visit-angers-church-officials.

May 30 and June 2.[119] I had no doubt in my mind that if it had been Black people attempting a coup, our bodies would have looked like McDonald's as they lay on the steps of the Capitol building that our enslaved ancestors built.[120] I wondered if my friend who thought the insurrection was an example of greatness could possibly understand how she sounded. It sent a chill down my spine to think that the same people who had insisted to me that "blue lives matter" were now cheering on these so-called patriots as they assaulted police officers. Not one of the Black people on the list of hashtags—the list that had brought me to my knees over the years—had ever even thought about assaulting an officer in this way, but they were dead. Black people could never have gotten away with something like this.

Never.

We almost never survive daring to confront America's wickedness on its own turf. Even when our only weapons are words, tears, cardboard fragments, and permanent markers. If it had been us, we would have never gotten so close as to look in the face of a Capitol police officer, let alone spit on, gnash our teeth near, or shout slurs at one. Whiteness made that day a spectacle rather than a massacre. I watched people wave Confederate flags and erect a lynching post. And just when I thought I couldn't be more sickened, a shirtless man wearing horns and a bearskin vest prayed in the chamber of the US Senate:

[119] Robert Hart, "Figures Show Stark Difference between Arrests at D.C. Black Lives Matter Protest and Arrests at Capitol Hill," *Forbes*, November 9, 2022, https://www.forbes.com/sites/roberthart/2021/01/07/figures-show-stark-difference-between-arrests-at-dc-black-lives-matter-protest-and-arrests-at-capitol-hill/?sh=41fedc225706.

[120] National Archives Public Affairs Staff, "National Archives to Display Pay Stubs of Slaves Used to Build U.S. Capitol and White House," National Archives and Records Administration, December 29, 2000, https://www.archives.gov/press/press-releases/2001/nr01-30.html.

Jesus Christ, we invoke your name: Amen! Let's say a prayer. Let's all say a prayer in this sacred space. Thank you, Heavenly Father, for gracing us with this opportunity to stand up for our God-given unalienable rights. Thank you, Heavenly Father, for being the inspiration needed to these police officers to allow us into the building, to allow us to exercise our rights, to allow us to send a message to all the tyrants, the communists, and the globalists that this is our nation, not theirs, that we will not allow the America—the American way, of the United States of America—to go down. Thank you, divine, omniscient, omnipotent, and omnipresent creator God, for filling this chamber with your white light and love, your white light of harmony. Thank you for filling this chamber with patriots that love you and that love Christ. Thank you, divine, omniscient, omnipotent and omnipresent creator God, for blessing each and every one of us here and now. Thank you, divine creator God, for surrounding (us) with the divine omnipresent white light of love and protection, peace and harmony. Thank you for allowing the United States of America to be re-born. Thank you for allowing us to get rid of the communists, the globalists and the traitors within our government. We love you and we thank you, in Christ's holy name we pray![121]

This was really happening. This white man was saying the "right things" about God—things most Christians would have said they believed. He talked about the brilliant "white" light of God and the holiness of God. He used the "omni" words that I'd learned from Wayne Grudem's popular evangelical book, *Systematic Theology*. He talked about "God-given rights" as he forcefully occupied the chambers of the Capitol with a gun by his side. And he got to go home to his family. Only a year earlier the cops arrived in riot gear to intimidate people who were there to proclaim their God-given value.

My ears were ringing.

The scenes from the Capitol played and replayed on the television all evening and into the next day. They continued into the day after that as cell phone videos emerged and authorities notified next of kin.

I couldn't stop the tears. I'd told my white friends for years what I was afraid the Trump presidency would embolden people to do. But they didn't believe me. They told me I was irrational. A white man followed me from the voting booth in 2016 in a Ford F-150 that had two Confederate flags mounted on the back of the cab. He was riding my bumper. I didn't know what else to do so I went live on my social media channel just in case something happened.

Still, a friend commented, "I think you are overreacting—it is just a flag; it doesn't mean he's racist or dangerous." That

---

[121] Jack Jenkins, "Jan. 6: A Timeline in Prayers," Religion News Service, January 7, 2022, https://religionnews.com/2022/01/06/jan-6-a-timeline-in-prayers/.

flag has stood for nothing but Black death and white terror for over a century of American history. In the last few years alone it inspired Dylan Roof to murder nine Black people at a church in Charleston, South Carolina, and Alex Fields, Jr. to drive his vehicle into a crowd in Charlottesville, Virginia. But *I* was "overreacting."

> I posted a lament about the insurrection on Facebook:
> I'm outraged. I'm disillusioned. And I do not give any f*cks about any apologies at this point. At this point, because it has been a decade of crying and pleading and forgiving and showing grace and having difficult conversations and forgiving and showing grace some more and being patient and walking the fine line of being nice and trying to be honest.

And these wrestlings were unrequited.

The effort was not reciprocated. I don't care about being nice right now. If I'm honest, I don't want anything to do with anybody white for a really long time.

Private messages began to pour in right away. But my stop-the-steal friend's stood out.

"Hey sister, I know you are hurting, but I think you were a little bit harsh. At the end of the day, even when we disagree, we are all on the same team. Let's keep it Kingdom."

Even though we had travelled as representatives of God's Kingdom together, the leaven of whiteness had convinced her that a few banners reading "Jesus 2020" makes a violent riot Christian.

Even when the banners are flying next to a noose.

The yeast of whiteness got in the way of my white friends' ability to tell the difference between the violent, hegemonic nationalism at the Capitol and what is actually true about God. Democracy is not a threat to God. But democracy can be a threat to whiteness. The insurrection was not the Kingdom coming. My white friends and I were not on the same team, and we hadn't been for some time.

It matters that Jesus was and will always be Jewish. Whiteness came to kill, steal, and destroy Jesus' context and rootedness in Palestine. White Jesus formed in the vacuum of the antisemitism that removed Jesus from the chosen people and bestowed God's special favor on Europe. The actions in the name of Jesus at the Capitol showed the world what it means to believe in a stolen election.

My friend's heartless response that day was the last straw. I was done. I didn't respond to her, or anyone. I closed my computer, and I went dark.

IV

PART FOUR

Black On My Own Time,
Woke on My Own Dime

I don't preach a social gospel; I preach the gospel, period. The gospel of our Lord Jesus Christ is concerned for the whole person. When people were hungry, Jesus didn't say, "Now is that political or social?" He said, "I feed you." Because the good news to a hungry person is bread.

— Archbishop Desmond Tutu[122]

I moved away from the ministry in Missouri thirteen months after Trayvon died. In the wake of the burgeoning Black Lives Matter movement, I wanted to be around people who felt the same pain and outrage as I did. I was done ignoring and abhorring my Blackness. I was suffocating, and the only thing I knew to do was start over in the Blackest place I could think of. So, in 2013, I began looking for jobs in Atlanta. The white ministry I joined in college was looking for a campus minister at an HBCU there. Despite my lingering reservations about white evangelicalism, it felt like my ticket out of Missouri.

---

[122] "Voice of the Day: Desmond Tutu." *Sojourners*, November 26, 2019. https://sojo.net/articles/voice-day-desmond-tutu-2.

I loved the job, and I loved my students. I was finally able to embrace Blackness and incorporate it into my discipleship and theirs. We talked openly about systems of injustice, and how BLM was an outlet for their raw emotions. I was finally embracing my race as a gift, and helping students do the same. I wanted them to recognize and own all that came with being Black: the fun, the pain, and the beauty. My goal was to help them understand it was impossible for us to be unapologetically Christian without being unapologetically Black. The two informed and influenced one another. I was convinced that we could not know the beauty of being Black unless we conversed with the one who chose our heritage for us. Neither could we authentically engage with truth without bringing our ethnic identities and cultural contexts to bear upon it. That first year of work and ministry was rewarding.

Then in 2014, a year after I arrived, Ferguson, Missouri went up in flames. My students were in tears, and the campus was filled with protests. Although my white ministry organization asked me to lead some of the campus demonstrations, I quickly realized that a mere geographical change had not been enough to liberate me from the leaven.

I kept having meetings about everything on the news with distraught students and I was doing my best to point them toward a Jesus who could help them, see them, and hear them. But it got harder and harder to do as I started to feel numb myself. The bodies and the brutality were too much. It took a toll on me.

That November, my regional ministry colleagues gathered for our annual planning conference. None of the white staff could tell that I was numb. We were in a Confederate state. We passed Confederate flags on the way to and from the mountaintop retreat location where we were expected to meet with God. The other Black staff and I were on edge that year because the grand jury were set to announce whether Officer Darren Wilson would be indicted for the murder of Michael Brown. We sat in the lobby of one of the retreat center buildings around a table waiting for the verdict. Finally, the moment came.

Officer Wilson was not going to face accountability.

At the exact moment of the announcement, the conference's director came out of the main meeting room to the table where all the Black staff were gathered. He stood directly in front of the TV and asked what was taking us so long to come join the team-building karaoke contest.

Whiteness always asserts that its priorities are more important than any other, no matter how trivial. Nothing was going to get in the way of the team-building exercise. Why couldn't we just close our eyes and participate? Why couldn't we be good sports? I was being expected in that moment to compartmentalize my Blackness and downplay the reality of what had just happened so that everyone could sing karaoke in peace.

I could weep for Michael Brown on my own time.

Yes, I had moved to Atlanta and surrounded myself with people who had skin like mine. But it took a minute to really start extracting the toxic whiteness in my worldview. I began to realize that all I was doing was trying to convince Black students that White Jesus loved them and didn't hate their Blackness, but that wasn't true. He did. He had no tolerance for who they were and never would. White Jesus cannot coexist with God or salvation any more than you can actually unleaven a loaf of bread. I was asking my Black students to try to eat around the poison because that's what I was doing. I was afraid to admit that the whole thing was putrid. I had only ever seen evangelical ministries center whiteness. I still thought it was the only food available, and I didn't want to starve. But I was starving in so many ways, and so were my students.

Black people's interests were not important unless they aligned with the ministry's. I was allowed to raise money to provide scholarships for Black students to attend the retreats at the tops of mountains lined with Confederate flags. But I was watching so many of them deal with unexpected financial challenges and family crises, and I couldn't raise money for *that*. I grew tired of helping students move out of their dorms because they couldn't afford the room and board anymore. What they wanted more than a retreat was to stay in school. Some of them were the very first in their families to go to college, but the disproportionate challenges they faced made it harder for them to finish.

So, in 2018 I decided to stop playing the middle. I left Atlanta and started my own nonprofit, a ministry dedicated to centering Black and marginalized college students, eradicating the barriers they face. My students helped me name it: Sub:Culture Incorporated. A subculture has interests at odds with the dominant culture. I had been offering students good news that was theoretical—White Jesus' strictly spiritual salvation. I wanted to offer students tangible demonstrations of God's love in a way that spoke to the value of their material lives. I did not want roadblocks to become dead ends for Black students living in a racialized world. White Jesus lived in harmony with antiblackness, and therefore could not love my students. They needed to meet the God who sees them, just like I did.

The Naughty List

What do the Scriptures say? How do you interpret them?

—Luke 10:26 (GNT)

A few years before I left Atlanta, I started reading the "naughty list" of authors that evangelicals deem deceptive and dangerous. Interestingly enough, only a few on the list were white.

I read Gustavo Gutiérrez, who believed that God spoke particularly to and through the poor and that the Bible could only be understood when seen from that perspective.[123] James Cone talked about how Jesus' experience in the first century was parallel to the Black experience in America.[124] Katie Cannon opened my eyes to womanist theology. She argues we must do the theological work that our souls must have when we experience tragedy. When we are desperate, like I was.[125] These authors offered me theological containers that could actually fit the carnage and confusion. *Why hadn't anyone told me about these voices?*

---

[123] Gustavo Gutierrez, *Theology of Liberation* (Scm Press, 2001).

[124] James H. Cone, *The Cross and the Lynching Tree* (Maryknoll, NY: Orbis Books, 2020).

[125] Katie G. Cannon, Sara Lawrence-Lightfoot, and Emilie M. Townes, *Katie's Canon: Womanism and the Soul of the Black Community* (Minneapolis, MN: Fortress Press, 2021).

What I found amongst these demonized theologians was a treasure trove of possibility that made sense of all those years of swallowing the lumps in my throat while chasing the fool's gold of white theology. All of them were angry about the same things as I was, and they still loved Jesus as much as I did. They made me realize there was nothing wrong with my Blackness, and I didn't have to give myself up to be loved by God. The more I gave space to my pain, my questions, and my doubts, the more aware I became of my nearness to God. I realized that God had always been in those places, and that it grieved him to see me reject so many parts of myself in the name of loving him. That's why my dad wrote me that email. That's why my grandmother called on election night. That's why my mother cried after I met White Jesus, and it's why my ancestors resisted.

At some point, I had subconsciously concluded that if Jesus was a white man, then I, a Black woman seeking to become like him, would have to deny and suppress the most beautiful and vulnerable aspects of my identity. This was the conundrum in my Christian discipleship: between me and White Jesus, one of us had to go. And it wasn't going to be me. Not this time. The naughty list was resurrecting me. It was White Jesus' turn to die.

Even though their perspective and experience were much closer to that of the actual, historical Jesus, my white, evangelical world scrutinized Black theologians more and took them less seriously. My white friends' social location—where they lived, who they surrounded themselves with, the sector of society they were accustomed to, being members in the dominant culture —had played into their reading, teaching, and interpretation of the text. But white theology can't name itself. The moment it does it ceases to be white theology. It assumes objectivity because it comes from a superiority complex created by white colonialists who monetized, legalized, and spiritualized whiteness. That's why it couldn't stretch and I couldn't breathe.

The folks who first took me down the Romans Road told me that the Bible was the highest authority because it was inerrant, infallible and inspired. The only way to take it seriously was to take it literally. And the only way to take it literally was to believe whatever they said about it. The white ministries and institutions I served in from that point on never once investigated the structure or culture or expectations of the tables they set. Whiteness caused them to believe that their theology was objective, and sound, and therefore biblical.

From that vantage point, any theology or experience that originated within a different social location was not worth serious examination. That's why the evangelical container White Jesus gave me couldn't handle the weight of all the dead Black bodies continually piled upon it. I wonder how I would have handled Trayvon had I known about Cone or Cannon. Losing sight of my inheritance as a Black woman kept me from the reality that was right in front of me.

The Bible cannot speak or interpret itself, and no one can read it bereft of their cultural lens. Too often, the Bible is a prop or an instrument to enforce the will of the wielder. And when the Bible is a prop, it can't be prophetic. But scripture, taken on its own terms, cannot be a weapon because it is too often confounding and mysterious.

And Jesus is *the* Word, made flesh.

My ancestors were not allowed to read or write, but they knew that what they were told about their lives and their worth was false. It didn't matter what the master told them the Bible said; they knew intrinsically that it was wrong. White slaveholders spoke in the name of the Bible in an effort to claim its authority and harness its power.

Believing in the inerrancy and clarity of scripture would have kept my family in chains. But they had courage to resist and confront harmful uses of scripture. Today, no one would dare question their rejection of slaveholders' "plain" reading of scripture. No one would say their intrinsic certainty that what was "clear" in the text was problematic in praxis, and thus wrong. The scripture said that slaves should obey their masters, but my ancestors knew from a different source that what they were experiencing in the name of Jesus had nothing to do with him. Coming to terms with that fact was the beginning of my enthusiastic return to scripture. In the secrecy of hush harbors, African slaves forged a purer faith than their white slaveowners. My ancestors were not converted to Christianity, but they converted Christianity to themselves! White preachers enslaved human beings, truncated the gospel, and weaponized scripture. But my ancestors came to Jesus without any social power to sanctify.

Scripture is littered with instances of God smiling upon disobedience of authority, and of scripture itself. Whether it's Puah and Shiphrah lying to preserve the lives of Hebrew babies,[126] or Rahab lying about where the Hebrew men were hiding[127] or David and his men eating the bread reserved for the

---

[126] Exodus 1:15–21

[127] Joshua 2:1-7

priests,[128] or Jesus healing on the Sabbath,[129] or Peter's deemphasis of the law in pursuit of gentile converts,[130] or Peter eating food sacrificed to idols.[131] The stories we tell, that we enjoy, that aid in our own liberation are often about people daring to believe that God is who they hoped God was. Scripture's authority in the lives of the oppressed lies in its ability to speak to, make sense of, and name their lived experience. Reading the naughty list freed me to see the inspiration of the scripture with new eyes.

Or maybe old ones. Because this is what I had fallen in love with when I first started reading the Bible. I loved the diversity of genres and perspectives. I loved Jesus' wit and mystery and curiosity. White Jesus made a desire for certainty overtake all that, and I stopped asking questions. By the time I was taking communion in the back pew of that Atlanta church, whiteness had clouded Jesus altogether. Extracting the leaven helped me take the Bible more seriously than I ever have because I let it be itself, and I stopped pretending I was objective. What the folks on the naughty list and my ancestors did was demand that theology *about* God be actually worthy *of* God.

And now, so do I.

---

[128] 1 Samuel 21:6; Matthew 12:4

[129] Luke 13:14

[130] Acts 15:5-11

[131] Acts 10:9-16; Acts 11:1-18

Get the Memo?

The second time I realized I hadn't moved far enough away from whiteness was in 2015, a year and a month after the grand jury refused to indict Darren Wilson for killing Michael Brown. The organization I worked for was holding a large missions conference. One of the keynote speakers clearly and boldly denounced the sin of whiteness from the main stage, and members of the worship band wore shirts proclaiming "Black Lives Matter." The Black staff at the conference felt vindicated and seen that night. It was as if the truth the preacher spoke that night put a fortification in our spirits. We cheered and clapped and shouted "preach!" We had all confronted the leaven in our days on staff with various ministries and churches, but it seemed like this organization was at least trying.

As usual, I took on the least coveted staff work assignment of the conference: intercessory prayer. They needed folks to serve night and day, and I had a bit of practice with that. During one shift I fell to the ground out of nowhere and wept uncontrollably. I didn't have any words for this travail. I was struck with a piercing sadness, grief, and pain. That's all I knew at the time. I learned later that this episode was around the same time major donors were announcing their decision to withhold financial investment in the organization because of what had happened on the main stage.

The conference was only an hour or so away from Ferguson. Some of us stayed behind after it ended and marched through Ferguson's streets. I was shocked to see that the memorial laden with balloons, teddy bears, and flowers was so small. We took a moment to put our feet on the sidewalk across from the area where Michael Brown died. Everything around that place where the Ferguson protests happened seemed so much larger on the news. But seeing its true size and learning about the donors' decisions made it click for me: blowing things out of proportion was a calling card of whiteness. And as I would soon find out, my ministry organization was about to follow suit.

Our leadership released a memo several months later that seemed to shake the earth. Christians who were openly "affirming"—meaning they believe that scripture affirms romantic, queer relationships instead of rejecting them as sinful—could no longer work for the ministry. The decision seemed so out of step with claims the ministry made about itself regarding creating welcoming communities and celebrating theological diversity. Among all the major, pressing issues in scripture, they chose this seemingly random point to demand doctrinal conformity from staff.

It was an intense time. The new policy forced many dear friends and colleagues out of their jobs. The ministry's decision made national news and loads of campus groups had to shut down in light of it. It put me and many of my colleagues in situations I'm not sure we were ready for. The ministry gave the staff time to come to a decision about where we stood. I told them I agreed with their stance. It was a lie. I wanted to keep my job. I didn't believe, but I behaved. And having staff who behave under the threat of losing their livelihood was both a predictable and acceptable state of affairs for the ministry.

I knew what I had been taught to do with students who had questions—which scriptures to show them, which prayers to pray. I knew how to cock my head and hold my smile so I didn't betray the fact that I was squirming and unconvinced. The fact of the matter was that my queer students were no more broken than my straight students. I never saw in them what I was always told I would. I often saw the Fruit of the Spirit in abundance, and the dissonance bothered me. I'd had my fill of coffee meet-ups sitting across from students who wanted to kill themselves because God would not make them straight. All I had to comfort them was a few Bible verses and a Frappuccino. These students were not trying to take over the world or force everyone to agree, they wanted there to be enough space for them. And frankly, they never caused anywhere near as much harm as the Calvinists in our community. They wanted to love God without shame. They wanted to have a family of their own someday, to be loved and share a life. I'd been telling them they didn't deserve any of that because of who they were, even though the blood of the ancestors who disbelieved their masters' interpretation of scripture ran through my African American veins.

The scripture was not "clear" on this issue. It never had been. But I was too afraid to go back and fix the damage I caused talking to all those queer students. I'd come back to myself in the sense that I wasn't going to deny my Blackness anymore in my pursuit of Jesus, but I had no idea how deeply I was infected with the whiteness I'd been imbibing. I had begun extracting it. I was reading the naughty list and focusing on ministry to Black students. But deep down, I still hated myself and I didn't know why. God had parted the Red Sea in front of me, but I hadn't moved. I was disconnected from my intuition. I was afraid. I didn't trust myself; I didn't trust anyone. Unearthing whiteness in my theology and learning about its history didn't restore the parts of myself that had succumbed to the poison. I felt like a failure and there was at least familiarity and safety in staying put.

I didn't know who I was apart from the persona I'd built in the white evangelical world. I'd made a name for myself. People were asking me to speak and lead more and more. I wasn't sure who I would be if I was anything else. I didn't even know if I had the stamina to create another life for myself. I was in my mid-thirties and the glimpses of Jesus I'd seen in the gospel narratives, though obscured, were real and they were potent. I figured that those crumbs would be enough to sustain me. On top of wanting to keep my job, my entire identity was built on the reputation of being a "solid" ministry leader with an unwavering faith and love for the scriptures. I didn't want to lose that either. So, I put pressure on myself to make sure all the quiet changes taking place in my perspective and theology wouldn't threaten my standing. That only fueled my drinking. And then I did something that I prayed would cure the numbness and validate my status as a faithful and reliable leader once and for all.

I went and got married.

V
PART FIVE

They Called It Love

Three months into my married life when my new husband threw the Christmas tree at me from across the room, I knew exactly who to call.

I was 19 when I met them. During my freshman year of college, at one of our weekly college ministry gatherings, the speaker was a white woman whose sons attended the group. She was intriguing to me; I was struck by how such a petite frame could carry so much conviction. After the gathering I summoned my courage, walked up to her, and shared how I could feel her wisdom through her words. I wanted to get together sometime.

She smiled and said, "That would be lovely. When would you like to meet?"

"A lot!" I said a little too eagerly. She laughed. We started meeting the next week and met every week after that until I graduated.

It was a mentoring and discipleship relationship, but it felt like more. She and her husband were like parents to me. Our relationship spanned two decades, four cities, and a million tears. She taught me to cook and clean, prayed for me to find my future husband, and bought me my first Bible concordance. I spent my birthdays and breaks around their quaint kitchen table. I brought friends from every city I lived in to that same table to experience the love and acceptance. The couple knew how much I loved Jesus, how much I wanted to be faithful, how much I longed to please God. I welcomed their instruction and correction; I valued their opinions above my own parents'. I listened to them more than I listened to myself. They even baptized me and performed part of my marriage ceremony. It felt to me like all the prayers they'd ever prayed for me worked, and they prayed for me relentlessly. I had no doubt their home would always be my home.

As a young adult I hadn't ever felt loved quite the way they made me feel loved. They were unphased by my phases in Calvinism and Charismania. They stayed and prayed through it all. For over ten years of my life, that table was an altar—the home itself a sanctum of love, kindness, and warmth. But the temperature started to change when Trayvon died.

I felt the shift for the first time when I joined that chorus of wounded souls who could do nothing but post a hashtag declaring that Black lives—our very own Black lives—mattered. It shook me when they told me I was making a mistake. It was so confusing to me that they of all people did not feel the ache I felt when I thought about how Trayvon went from carrying Skittles to fighting for life. I ignored the hurt and convinced myself that we could agree to disagree.

I tried to make my outrage more palatable by sprinkling it with Christianese phrases like "wrestling with" and "grieving my heart," instead of telling the truth that I was filled with rage. "Struggling with the world" was code for indignance. "Having a hard time" diluted the fact that I was depressed and despondent. "I just need the Lord to give me his heart" covered up my absolute fury with the mental acrobatics of my white friends.

They continued to see me "wrestle" with so many things. Each new instance brought its own placating, "Release it to the Lord." They told me, "God doesn't see color, and neither should we." When I questioned God, they reiterated that he was in control.

A month before the tree incident, I told them my husband was calling me names and I was starting to feel really depressed. They told me that I was "wrestling with my flesh" and that being a submissive wife could not be accomplished by human might or power, only by the Spirit of God. That's why it should not have been a surprise that their response to my frantic Christmas Eve phone call was to ask me *what the reason was that he gave for throwing a tree at me.*

"Well, he lost his job again and I was considering taking the PlayStation I got him back so we could pay rent. He told me I ruined his Christmas, so he was going to ruin mine."

They asked me if I had prayed about going back on my purchase before I told him. They reminded me of the biblical entreaty to "Let your yes be yes,"[132] which to them was an instruction to be sure of your decisions and to not change your mind after the fact.

About a year later, I was sitting in my car in a bowling alley parking lot. I was hoping I could finish up before he got there.

I'd checked all the things off my to-do list. The students had arrived. I'd passed out the tokens and tickets, and they had already headed into the bowling alley. I wish I could remember

---

[132] Matthew 5:37

everything about that night, but I can't. I can only remember what happened when he arrived. He parked behind me; I am still unsure if he did that intentionally to catch me "in the act." He liked doing that sort of thing.

"What is that in your hand?!" he barked.

"Please," I said, "not now; it has been a long day. Please don't."

One thing I do remember is how the air felt. It was calm and silent, and I suppose that's why I snuck out of the bowling alley for my cigarette break. I loved smoking, but I pretended I didn't. Good Christian leaders didn't do that sort of thing. Neither did Proverbs 31 women for that matter. The truth was that I liked the way the filter made a crunch sound when I activated the menthol. I loved the tangy heat that nestled on my tongue when I took a drag, and the way the warmth enveloped my chest like I was holding frozen hands over a small fire. The gray strands of smoke seemed to dance to the rhythm of my thoughts as I savored the nicotine. It was a secret ritual for me, sacred and serene.

He broke in on the dance of my thoughts by walking up to my open window and yelling.

"You are so disgusting! I don't want to be with a smoker. I told you that!" The nestled heat made its escape, and I turned my head away so as not to blow it in his face.

It didn't matter.

I was looking the other way, so I didn't know what hit me. I just knew it hurt. He knocked the cigarette out of my hand with so much force that my wrist popped from the impact. I grimaced.

"Great. Now, I can't bowl," I thought, and began rolling up my window. I felt an emotional connection to the glass as I watched it glide upward. It reminded me of the walls I had slowly erected on the inside over the past year of marriage.

My relationship was getting steadily worse, but I tried to convince everyone it was getting better. I even tried to convince myself.

"I only do these things because I love you, Tamice."

He called it love because he didn't know any better.

And neither did I.

There was a lot more I needed to unleaven.

I was 32 when I got married, which in Christian purity culture years is about 62. I had proudly dedicated my twenties to the Lord, and church people seemed alright with that. But now it had been two years of side glances and what's-your-types. I had even begun calling my closet ROY G. BIV because I had bridesmaids dresses in every hue.

Moreover, the more I spoke up about Black lives, the more people questioned my character and devotion. I still wanted to prove to them that I loved Jesus, and that it was possible to combine faith with advocacy for Black lives. But in White Jesus' world, singleness was more than just loneliness; it was a mark of either God's displeasure or my need to mature into a suitable wife. By that point, I'd done missions work foreign and domestic. I'd led ministries and worship teams. I had preached on a subway in Boston. I had stopped speaking for 21 days in response to reading a single verse in Isaiah. I felt as though I'd leveled up my discipleship as high as I could. So, what was left to do? The end goal, I gathered from the lives of ministry leaders, was to marry, have children, and get a nice house (that of course we would use to host small groups as a "thank you" to Jesus for the blessing). We would go to church every Sunday morning and Bible study every Wednesday night. We'd get a dog, and then have a baby and post one of those cute announcement photos on Instagram. After that I don't know what, but people would definitely look at us and say we were "on fire for God."

Getting married was my last attempt at making White Jesus work. I was too tired to keep walking in the direction of the freedom I was discovering because it was so lonely and scary and costly. I still longed for familiarity, certainty, and control over the narrative about my life. I chose the man I married; I wasn't tricked. I believed married life would distract me from the pain of disillusionment. It would rescue my reputation and vindicate all those years of singleness. Being married was going to catapult me to a new level of spiritual achievement. And maybe people—especially my mentor couple—wouldn't think I was too liberal anymore.

Of all the poison the leaven of whiteness pumped into my life, none was harder to recognize or remove than the self-hatred. My husband treated me the way White Jesus said I, as a sinner, deserved. *I had been taught that marriage was hard. And it was about holiness, not happiness. I was supposed to sacrifice. I was supposed to suffer. Life was not about my enjoyment.* I stayed because I thought I had to.

I endured narcissistic abuse for nearly two years straight and couldn't call it what it was. I was afraid to trust my instinct that it was wrong, and I wanted to show that I wasn't too progressive to submit to authority. Besides, I blamed myself. I chose this. I deserved these consequences. And getting divorced would only be more of a reason for white people to dismiss what I was saying about racism, whiteness, or Donald Trump.

So, the night he slammed on the brakes to teach me not to talk back, I recited Bible verses in my head about the destructive power of angry words and stayed silent. The inertia had thrust me forward so hard I was sure I would miscarry from the impact. He was hungry, and apparently, I had taken too long coming down the stairs. Still, I let it slide.

"Nobody has to know," I thought, "any day now this will all be better. He will get better. I'm so early on in the pregnancy; only a few people will know if I lost the baby." I climbed back into my seat. "I know he didn't mean it Lord," I whispered to myself. "Please, help me to see what you see, Lord, and love what you love. And please God protect this baby."

The following Saturday, when the cramps came, I was admitted to the hospital. The doctor said I'd lost the baby and the internal bleeding he saw on the ultrasound was now threatening my life. But when I came to, the surgeon apologized for performing an unnecessary surgery. She confessed they didn't know what happened. Several doctors reviewed the images before they cut me open, but once they got in there, there was no bleeding. They eventually found my baby, still alive and right where she was supposed to be.

We went home, but not for long. A series of scares and tests followed. The doctors deemed the pregnancy high-risk, and I landed in the hospital long term. It was a reprieve from the situation at home. At least in the hospital, the duress was minimal.

One nurse recognized the signs. She constantly asked me if I was okay and left domestic abuse hotline information laying around for me after her shifts. On one occasion, she even had security escort my husband out of the hospital room. He had yelled and thrown fruit snacks at me because the TV in the room didn't have ESPN. She wanted to ban him from coming back, but I convinced her he was just having a stressful day and it was his favorite team he was missing. Knowing I was a Christian, she confided in me that she was as well. She told me three things: that my baby was going to be okay, that she struggled to see how what she had witnessed could come from God, and that I would understand her concerns when I was a parent.

Shopping Carts

There were nearly 300 people at my wedding in September of 2016. It was extravagant and we carefully planned every detail. The venue and weather were amazing. It couldn't have been more perfect as far as weddings go. Everyone I loved was in one place at one time for one reason, and I was nowhere to be found.

Dissociation.

Apparently, it is my superpower.

I went to therapy after the bowling alley incident, and this tendency of mine to dissociate came to light for the first time. My therapist, Dr. Hanna,[133] was a sweet white woman who dressed like Lorelai Gilmore. She grew up Christian but didn't identify as one anymore. I wasn't sure she would understand what was happening to me, but she was cheap, and I was broke. Plus, she'd done her thesis on Religious Trauma.

At our first session, I told her that I had stopped going to church at one point. When we started dating, my future husband said he wanted to be my spiritual leader and it was time for me to start going back. But anytime I attended certain events, heard certain songs, or listened to certain preachers, I got hives, itched uncontrollably, and felt like I couldn't breathe.

---

[133] Dr. Hanna is not the therapist's real name.

Afterward, I felt like I was outside myself, had a hard time sleeping, and became depressed.

"I think I am having a nervous breakdown," I told her. She jumped right in.

"What can you tell me about the day you got married?"

It was not the question I expected, but I answered. I remembered karaoke and the bachelorette party. I remembered the late-night conversation with my bridesmaids. I remembered sitting in the garage the morning of and crying. I remembered seeing my brothers after I was dressed.

"After that it's just … blank."

"So, what I hear you saying is you weren't at your own wedding."

I gasped, "I wasn't at my own wedding!"

"Mmm hmm. Let's sit with that." She smiled a knowing smile; I would see that same smile a lot more over the course of our time together. She let me ponder. Why couldn't I remember anything? Why were all the faces blurry when I tried? I didn't remember dancing or eating. I didn't remember saying my vows, and I couldn't recall anything from my honeymoon.

"Have you ever heard of neural pathways?" she asked.

"No, what's that?"

That was when Dr. Hanna talked to me about shopping carts.

She explained that neural pathways are like tracks in our brains. When our brains receive consistent messages over an extended period of time, they create these tracks. Dr. Hanna told me that what I was experiencing was normal:

You've been told messages that were reinforced in your life experience and in your religious experiences. These messages have created tracks in your brain. It sounds to me like the things you are experiencing as a result of leaving and reconsidering these religious ideas are creating a lot of anxiety for you. Think about a shopping cart with a broken wheel. When you begin to think critically and challenge ideas and beliefs that you've held for a long time, it can feel a lot like trying to maneuver a shopping cart with a broken wheel. The anxiety and the weariness you feel could be coming from the effort it takes to push the cart on a new track. You veer when you don't want to. You get frustrated. What people don't understand about these pathways is we can create new ones. We just have to be patient with the faulty wheel, and it will eventually settle into the new track that your brain will create to accommodate it. You have done a lot of this work around your thinking about God and what you know to be true in light of the issues facing the Black community, but I am wondering how much work you've done in terms of the way you think about yourself? I would love for us to do some of that work if you are feeling ready and up for it.

Before we finished our session that day Dr. Hanna said, "You know Tamice, it sounds like your love for God and God's love for you is just fine. Have you ever thought that maybe God is trying to speak to you through your body? Is it possible that while your mind is creating new paths Jesus might be talking to you in a different way? Why don't you try paying attention to that and see what happens."

"Pay attention to my body?

"Yes." She replied, "your body has been a part of your journey and it sounds like there may be things it has been trying to tell you for a little while. Listen to it, it's not your enemy."

"Ok, so what do I say to it?"

"Nothing" she said. "Just listen and let it speak for a change."

After committing to several more sessions, I went home and closed my eyes. It had been a long time since I had paid any attention to my body.

And it had some things to say.

Flying

In Jesus' worldview, he laid to waste the fallacies of Platonic dualism that exist in our modern era and that presume the earth or the body or anything earthly is less spiritual than the mind, the spirit, or things more abstract. To Jesus, as it should be to us, the earth is wholly spiritual, as are our bodies.

—Randy Woodley[134]

The last time I had felt connected to my body was the same day I got my superpower. I don't remember much. Just the scratchy dusty carpet on the back of my neck and the weight holding me down. I didn't look at his face; I turned my head and stared at the green vintage lamp that reminded me of the 1970s. The glow of the TV was on my right and the bottom of the couch on my left. I hadn't kissed anyone before, and if this was kissing, I didn't like it at all. I was 10 or 11. He was older and bigger than me, and I kept hoping for someone to come into the room and rescue me. I could hear the muffled sounds of music and the adults laughing and drinking in the other room. They

134 Randy Woodley, "The Fullness Thereof," in *Keeping the Faith: Reflections on Politics & Christianity in the Era of Trump & Beyond*, ed. Jonathan P. Walton, Suzie Lahoud, and Sy Hoekstra (Middletown, DE: KTF Press LLC, 2020), pp. 189-195, 191.

couldn't hear me, and I am not even sure if I cried for help out loud or not. Inside I was screaming. I hated the way he invaded my space and how he handled my body. But I couldn't fight, and I couldn't get up. That was the day I learned to fly.

Flying was so safe—I didn't have to hear or see or feel anything. It felt so much better than whatever was happening to that girl lying down there on the floor, 20 feet below me as I sat suspended in the air. I got so good at flying that at times I didn't even know I was doing it. By the time I met White Jesus in high school, I could hold entire conversations, do my homework, or even speak to an audience without anyone knowing I was floating above it all, watching from a distance.

Most people never checked whether I was really present. And when I started going to White Jesus' church, my superpower became laudable. Since feelings were not welcome in the realm of serious Christianity, my ability to ignore and suppress them was a mark of maturity. I learned quickly that I wasn't going to be safe or taken seriously in White Jesus' church, but no matter, I could always fly away.

When the whole world started wearing masks, I was only just beginning to take mine off. I was finally being honest with myself about what my marriage was doing to me. But every time I questioned the decision I made to keep saying "yes" to my ex, I thought about the embarrassment I would feel if people knew what I had agreed to experience behind closed doors. At times I truly thought I might snap. Other times, I wanted to die. But I couldn't come up with a legitimate reason to leave. I felt I needed a higher purpose, something to spin, some biblical way to explain leaving, and I didn't have one. He hadn't beaten me, and he hadn't cheated. People thought of me as strong, so

I felt I should be able to tough it out. Plus, my parents spent so much money on that wedding. I didn't want to disappoint them again with another bad decision.

Dr. Hanna was right, all those excuses, all that shame, and the arguments against advocating for myself were like faulty wheels on a shopping cart. They were not loud; they were subtle and persistent. White Jesus loves those faulty wheels because they ward off the disruption of freedom. It was easy to treat them as the voice of the Holy Spirit before I unleavened because my zeal and efforts to follow White Jesus had erased my common sense and self-worth. The only way I knew how to deal with the faulty wheels was to fly.

But then Harlym was born.

Birth and Rebirth

I dreamt of Harlym. From the moment she existed I knew her. I felt her. She gave me a sort of hope that there was something good inside me, that something good could come from me. She was aiding and abetting the growing internal resistance to the messages I was getting from my husband and White Jesus. It's no wonder there were so many obstacles to her birth. There were just as many to my rebirth, which she set in motion.

The high-risk pregnancy meant doctors pricked me with needles a hundred times on every area of my body where a vein might be. I spent more hours than I can count bound to a bed that monitored and restricted every movement. After my unnecessary emergency surgery, I went home to my miserable home life.

As my husband and I pulled up to an appointment with the high-risk specialist a month later, he slammed my hand in the door and sped off before I could get my bag out of the car. It was to teach me another lesson about something I don't remember. The specialist ended up admitting me, and I stayed there until Harlym came. She was born almost three months premature.

For 81 days while she fought for life in the NICU, I fought to keep my dignity at home. We brought her home from the hospital and the very next month I moved us in with my family.

Harlym was three months old and weighed only eight pounds. I felt it would be safer with family. I didn't know if she and I would survive by ourselves. I wanted Harlym to see and to know love that, even if it was imperfect, was at least there.

But it turns out it is harder to abuse someone when they aren't isolated. After four months in my parents' home, we moved up the road to an apartment building. The neighbors in the complex witnessed the fighting. When he was gone, one neighbor I'd met on the elevator would come to see me and Harlym. She never said much about the situation except when she would leave.

"Don't forget. God can make a way out of no way."

I saw her on the balcony the day I took Harlym and left for good. She folded her hands as if to say she was praying and proud of me. She watched until I drove away.

After my divorce was final, I reached back out to Dr. Hanna. I wrote to her and thanked her for helping me reunite with my body. So many things in my past made sense now. I told her that my baby girl had finally done something no one had ever been able to do. She made me quit flying.

I told her it was coming back to my body that made the difference. And Harlym showed me how strong and majestic my body could be. I'd brought a human into the world. I was thankful for my body and began thinking of ways to be better at honoring it.

I told Dr. Hanna about the night I left for good.

"He told my baby girl to call me a piece of shit."

She knew that wasn't the first time he'd called me that, and she also knew I had never corrected him. So, I explained.

My body had a strong, visceral reaction to hearing it when my 18-month-old did in fact say "Mommy, you're a piece of shit."

That's what did it. I could have flown right then, but there was my baby girl, looking right at me with no idea of what she had just said. And I hadn't moved. My feet were still on the ground. I decided I was going to build and live a life where Harlym would never have to fly.

My nurse said I would understand when I was a parent, and my neighbor said God could make a way.

They were both right.

Downhill From Here

By the time I got divorced in 2020, I could count the number of white friends I had left on one hand. Our conversations had grown fewer and further apart on the heels of Trump's inauguration. But on an unusually cold night in January 2018, I travelled to be in the wedding of one of the last ones. I was pregnant (I remember because I really wanted a drink). I rode to the rehearsal dinner with the bride-to-be and her mom. We took a shortcut through the "bad part of town."

Her mom looked at me and said, "We are in your neck of the woods now. If anything happens say 'yo yo yo' or something so they know we are with you." My friend said nothing. I was relieved when we arrived at the restaurant.

As I sat down next to the mentor couple I'd had since college, I overheard them saying, "He might be a little rough around the edges, but at least he tells it like it is. Antifa and BLM *are* dangerous terrorist groups. He's the only man with enough guts to say it."

I was staggered.

I was also staying at their house that night. On the ride there, I told them I'd overheard their conversation and that Black Lives Matter is not a terrorist group. I finally spoke about the deep feelings of hurt I felt because of their reaction to my grief over Trayvon's death.

"Which one was Trayvon again?"

My ears were ringing. My teeth hurt. They knew me; they loved me. I shook my head. *They just needed perspective*, I told myself. I tried to explain the anger and rage I'd felt for so long. I spoke of the silence of the church and the white community that had betrayed me. I told them that the hashtag was holy and had taken on spiritual significance for many Black Christians, including me. I told them that Jesus had to care about Black lives and that those lives didn't hold the same value as the lives of White people in America. I talked about all that I had learned about Trayvon's case, about the laws and history and biases that undergirded the brutality that took his life and all the others. I talked about the fact that their theology was missing crucial perspectives of people whose backgrounds and worldviews were more similar to Jesus'. I told them about Constantine, and the politics of orthodoxy, and the importance of Jesus' ethnic identity. I even told them about my tequila sunrise services and the day the silence broke. I tried to convince them that the horrific realities of whiteness would not vanish on their own, and since we loved Jesus, it was our job to expose them.

After all that, their response was, "Make sure you're careful, Tamice. That BLM group was started by three lesbian Marxists." I decided I was done pretending, and I think they could hear it in my silence. I wanted to scream at them, "you told me not to vote for Obama! You told me he was the Antichrist! And you support this man?!"

We stared at each other a few more moments before she broke the silence: "Well for us it's really about Mike Pence. He's a man of God and we truly only voted for Trump because of him." When they parked, I got out of the car and ran inside to the restroom. My tears were hot and fiery. I was breathing heavily. I told them it was a cold. Although I continued to love them dearly, after that night we held each other at arm's length. I only had two more significant conversations with them: one when I told them I was ending my marriage, and one after that when I fell in love.

That last conversation was in 2021. I could tell as soon as she picked up the phone that it would be our last.

"Hello?"

"Hey! I know it has been a while. I wanted to tell you guys about some things that have been happening for me."

"Oh, we've known for quite some time now. We were told a while ago."

"Oh, you know already?"

"Yes."

"Who told you?"

"That's not what matters here, Tamice."

"Is that why you haven't answered my calls?"

"Well, we wanted to speak to you in person about our decision. But time has not permitted. Surely you aren't terribly surprised, Tamice. You know us. You know we can't fellowship with you when you are actively living in sin. We are going to have to break relationship as the Bible directs us to do."

"I'm not living in sin; I'm living for the first time. I am really happy, and I still love Jesus and we are fine. Me and Jesus are fine, and the scripture has never been more alive to me. Honestly."

"We love you Tamice, you know that, but the scripture is clear. We cannot have fellowship with you anymore."

"Everybody keeps saying they love me lately. Right before they stop talking to me. If this is love, I want whatever came before it. I thought y'all were my friends. You guys are like my family. I didn't realize that I was so disposable to so many people. Will I ever see you guys again?"

"Well, a lot of us have been concerned about you for quite some time now. With you going on ad nauseum about Critical Race Theory, your decision not to fight for your marriage, and now this—surely you can't be surprised that you've lost so many people."

I didn't think I could feel worse pain than I felt when we hung up. It seems strange now, but I actually wondered whether I was dreaming. When I realized I wasn't, the grief enveloped me like thick quicksand. Had they always been this way? Was I only just realizing it now because I had stopped flying? How could they be so sure it was right to cut me off? Why couldn't they err on the side of love? Did they ever know me? Couldn't they see the hypocrisy of rejecting someone in the name of Jesus when that person is doing everything they can to follow his example? Did they think Jesus died on the cross to make their relationships conditional? I thought I meant more to them. I should have known I didn't when they dismissed my use of the BLM hashtag as a lapse in judgement, or when they forgot who Trayvon was.

I tried to tell them I wasn't in sin; I was just happy. I knew the scriptures as well as they did, they'd taught me to love them, in fact. The wage of sin is death, but I had never, ever been more alive than this.

It didn't matter.

White Jesus performed a miracle that day. He made 20 precious years vanish in one 13-minute phone call. Neither this couple nor any of the other people I lost were expendable to me, but I wasn't willing to sacrifice myself on the altar of their comfort anymore. I don't know if you've ever been "handed over to the devil" before, but it isn't awesome.

I never even got to tell them the story of what happened.

VI
PART SIX

FAITH UNLEAVENED

Fear Goes First

Let my people go, so that they may worship me in the wilderness.

—Exodus 7:16 (NIV)

White Jesus made me forget who I was and convinced me that the forgetting was a sign of maturity. After all, I was supposed to decrease as Christ increased in me. But all White Jesus really "increases" is dread. I was terrified of being anything White Jesus didn't want me to be. The fears were endless: fear of Hell, fear of judgement, fear of rejection, fear of leading people astray, fear of getting doctrines wrong, fear of sinning, fear of losing community, fear of losing credibility.

And even though I felt that so many things were wrong with White Jesus, I was afraid that if I pulled on any individual string of my faith, the whole thing would come unraveled, and all my fears would come true at once. If I listened to my gut instead of the preacher on one thing, what would that say about everything else? What would happen to every other belief I'd clung to so tightly? I had built my entire life on top of those beliefs. Letting go of beliefs feels like death, or at the very least, a wasted life. What person would give them up? Who volunteers to lose their whole life?

These fears were all based in future possibilities, though, and for me, the present, concrete realities of grief and mourning as a Black person in America ended up being stronger and more urgent. This is why I say Trayvon started my journey of salvation. Salvation wasn't about leaving my body for eternity, but coming back to it in the here and now.

After I let go of the fear and stepped into freedom, I continued to find deep resonance with the book of Exodus. The wilderness must have felt exciting to the mixed multitude that followed Moses out of Egypt. They were finally free. Emerging from the chaos of the Red Sea, the Hebrew refugees confronted a calm and palpable humility. A people enslaved to the empire their whole lives now had an invisible God with more power than the tyrant they used to serve, and this God was serving them.

A fire by night.

Light in darkness and warmth in the cold.

A cloud by day.

A shield in the scorching sun and oppressive arid heat.

Manna from heaven.

Unleavened sustenance for the journey.

He truly served his people. Masters don't serve slaves. Gods don't usually show concern for the people themselves, but what they might produce. Gods don't traverse a dusty desert with newly emancipated slave folk. A real king would be embarrassed to take such a lowly position among such a lowly people.

On the edge of the wilderness outside white evangelicalism, I too felt free. And what's more, I felt like God was serving me. I experienced relief, like a weight had been lifted. I could see all of God's activity in my life bringing me to that point. I was finally allowed to reject harmful theology, to not know, to think critically, to use common sense, and to listen to myself. Jesus (the real one) was not suppressing who I was. He met my needs and showed me my value.

But when it was time to walk that freedom out into the unknown, I realized the atrophy that had taken place while I was in bondage to whiteness. I didn't know how much energy it would require to rest in freedom. I'd been in a traumatized survival mode for so long and for so much of my life. The rawness that accompanied the new embrace of freedom was both thrilling and frightening. All the fears were falling away. At the same time, when I experienced the rejection and the loss of my old friends, it hurt so deeply, and I felt it all the more acutely because I was paying attention to my feelings. In many ways, I felt like a newborn baby just beginning to live—seeing and hearing and experiencing the world for the first time. I wondered if this was what Jesus meant when he told Nicodemus he must be born again to enter the kingdom.[135]

Simultaneously, there was a war on the inside of me as I put effort into creating new neuropathways. People questioned my devotion, my salvation, and my fitness for ministry. It wasn't easy to wade through the weight of their assumptions and hurtful words. They made me second guess myself a lot at first. There were so many reminders of the pain that I had avoided by conforming to their expectations. But God was committed to my freedom.

The Hebrews left Egypt with a God whose love and obsession with freedom is real and potent. In the wilderness, God's

---

[135] John 3:5

passion pressurizes and becomes to the Hebrews a mirror, a blessing, and sometimes a thorn. It isn't far into the wilderness when the refugees learn that the unleavened bread they made for their journey was a metaphor for who they were supposed to become.

A person in survival mode is difficult to save. God had led them out, but they had to learn how to live unchained. They'd become accustomed to a certain routine way of being, even though their portion in life was oppressive. Living free in the wilderness exposed that they desired familiarity and predictability. but those are not always facets of freedom. What was out there in the wilderness was scary and unknown, and the vulnerability of it all was jarring. Anything new, even if it was better, took courage to embrace.

They complained often about their circumstances. Something in the wilderness was always exposing or confronting their fear,[136] insecurity,[137] pride,[138] or their greed.[139] All of which if not dealt with would make them just like the empires around them. They were meant to be different. Unleavened. Theirs would be a kingdom of priests, not tyrants. This kingdom would be marked by worship and humility, hospitality and generosity.

I think of the Hebrews often and what it must have been like to have been born into Egyptian slavery. They were in survival mode from day one; they didn't have a choice. Sure, they heard stories about a time when things were not like this.

---

[136] Numbers 14:1-4

[137] Numbers 20:2

[138] Numbers 12:1

[139] Numbers 11:4-6

Stories about patriarchs and promises on mountaintops, but their everyday existence was so far from that. I imagine what it must have been like to wake up in the middle of the night and prepare the first Passover meal. How risky must it have felt? What if Moses had been wrong about what was coming? What if someone had seen or heard all the commotion? What if the whole thing had been a test or a trick? They must have had so much faith in the old stories and the testimonies they heard and the power of the plagues they saw. It would have taken so much for them to not only hope for something better, but to believe that they deserved something better. And even more than that, to believe that God agreed with them.

My experience with white evangelicalism was similar. It was toxic in so many ways, but it also offered me something. It made the world simple and straightforward. There was us and there was them. People were either saved or not, and we knew who was who. Light and truth were found here, evil and darkness were over there. I knew that sin and righteousness were incompatible and never the two shall meet. Whiteness creates binaries. Its entire purpose is to separate and categorize people and cultures according to a hierarchy. It's evil, but evil can comfort, in its own perverted way.

If it hadn't been for that reminder from God to remember the bread of life, White Jesus might've killed me dead. But God spoke to me. He revealed to me that it was time to leave, and the leaven couldn't come where I was going. Years later, I was finally out, but what comes after the initial thrill of the escape? When you try to trust Jesus with the parts of your life you had boarded up, what happens to all your coping mechanisms that you developed when you were living in fear?

I realized that God's love without condition—the love that White Jesus often talks about but never demonstrates—is extremely confrontational. That unconditional love of our entire self mirrors our bias, indifference, and inconsistency back to us. That was another thing I fell in love with when I first read Jesus' story in the gospels. He spoke truth in love to show liberation and acceptance to anyone bound by anything, whether it was "Go and sin no more,"[140] or "Your sins are forgiven,"[141] or "I do not condemn you,"[142] or "Pray for your enemies,"[143] or "Turn the other cheek."[144]

Egypt was the breadbasket that required the nations to come to its land to receive what it had. God led the Hebrews in the opposite direction: they took what they had and went out to share it with the world. "In you the families of the earth will be blessed"[145] is what God said to them. Those who joined in their story of freedom and salvation would eat the same unleavened bread. The gods of the empires served the will of kings. The Hebrews worshiped Yahweh who was fierce and free, a critic of kings and an advocate for vulnerable, oppressed people. God wanted the Hebrews to share with the world a salvation that wasn't just about escaping hell. He wanted people to believe that it is possible to feel secure and alive at the same time—that you can be free with no fine print. Or as Jesus put it, "If the Son sets you free, you will be free indeed."[146]

[140] John 8:11
[141] Luke 7:48
[142] John 8:10
[143] Matthew 5:44
[144] Matthew 5:38
[145] Genesis 22:18
[146] John 8:36 (NIV)

When God calls Israel into the wilderness, it is because a fundamental shift must take place in their theology and their understanding of who God is. They need to be in a barren land to learn that their God will make bread fall from the sky if they need it—that they are no longer slaves because he is not a slave master. They had to become people who could imagine that God can make water come out of rocks, that the wilderness can be an oasis.

That anything is possible.

The Exodus is nothing without the wilderness. The wilderness teaches us that life is bitter and sweet, hard and simple. Rest and shalom aren't only out there somewhere in the Promised Land. They are where we are now, because God is with us. It teaches us that things aren't always either/or, but sometimes both. Truth and even life can be found in tragedy, and beauty can come from ashes. The richness of a feast at a table in a safe land is not about the bread, but who is at the table as the bread is broken. And exodus is not the only aim of God.

The point of my exodus, my liberation from whiteness, was the wilderness. I had to learn to trust myself. I had to learn to let go of the fear of failure or divine rejection. I had to be free to believe that God was actually kind, actually just, actually merciful, and that I could actually trust him with my deepest pain. I could replace the need for certainty with the unrestricted reality of liberation and love.

And once I went through that, I found that the wilderness was always meant to end in worship.

Wild

I had done so much work in therapy and had come to a restful place. The journey to get there was tumultuous, but I felt free, or at least as free as I could be. I was settling into an inconvenient life as a single mom, but at least I was giving my daughter a life and a chance at her own freedom.

I was still working hard on staying in my body and listening to my emotions. One day, I was watching the finale episode of the first season of a TV series called *The Wilds* when something I never could have expected suddenly happened.

Two female characters, Toni and Shelby, kissed, and the Holy Spirit spoke to me.

"Who told you you were naked?" And then a thought: "A person who doesn't look in the mirror will never see themselves."

I felt something as I watched the kiss, and I suddenly found myself transported to the first time I felt the same way.

I was six.

One after one, parts of my life began to flash before my eyes—things that I now recognized indicated I didn't feel the same way as the girls around me when it came to boys. The walls of my room remained bare while my friends covered every inch of theirs in posters of heartthrobs. I never grew out of being a "tomboy." I saved notes from specific female friends. I was highly successful in the purity culture of my old churches, and never seemed to feel the temptations that the youth leaders obsessed over.

In many memories, especially those before I started flying, I recalled knowing that what I felt was different. Not weird or bad or nasty. It felt like curiosity.

It just was what it was.

Learning to fly kept the questions these feelings might have provoked from coming to the surface. And White Jesus buried the feelings too. Nobody knew about them, not even me. But now here we were, the Spirit and I, unleavening even more as I said it out loud.

"Oh shit, I'm gay."

I told a few people my revelation, but mostly kept it to myself. I had a daughter to raise, and Sub:Culture, my only source of income, had mostly evangelical donors. Still, curiosity and the isolation of COVID quarantine drove me to dating apps. After a week or two, I realized that I hated the perpetual small talk, that I was too Jesus-y for the non-Christian dating apps, and that none of the Christian apps had a queer option. What I truly longed for was community and understanding, as if that would be proof that God hadn't given up on me. My friend sent me a text: "have you heard of this one?"

I opened the text and clicked on the link. It was an ad for an app where LGBTQ+ Christians could find connection, belonging, and love. On this app you could find friends as well as dates, and it matched people based on values. I logged in using a fake name, just in case I bumped into someone I already knew. The app matched people once a week. It was in its beta phase, so the first week it didn't work. The next week, right before going to bed, I remembered to check the app. I had six messages waiting, but it was the one on the bottom that caught my eye. I saw the word *resonate,* and it piqued my curiosity. I could see their name, but due to another glitch I couldn't see their face.

"Hi, I saw your profile and what you wrote really resonated with me. I'd love to connect if you're interested."

When I clicked their profile, it said they "believe the promises of the brown refugee who said the first shall be last and follow me."

Hell yes, I was interested. Even though I couldn't see their face.

They were authentic and made me feel safe. They made me laugh and think, and they loved asking questions as much as I did. It felt like we were collaborating on a journey of selves, reflecting our own and the other's worth back to one another.

When they talked about Jesus, I felt a familiarity that was hard to describe. They had been hurt too, for different reasons, but they were in the same predicament as I was. They wanted community, but were not willing to lose sight of themselves in their relationship with Jesus or others. We'd both concluded before we met that it must be possible to be a queer Christian because, well, here we were. They were funny and kind. They loved logic puzzles and math. They were extremely family-oriented just like me. They loved to bake and hike and read.

They made my heart move and that was new.

We talked about the shenanigans at the Capitol and the murder of George Floyd. We talked about our scars and our pet peeves. We talked about Trayvon, a lot.

They told me they had a passion for mental health and ASL.

I told them I loved being Black and wasn't going to downplay any parts of myself anymore. They said they weren't interested in someone who would. It felt like I had dreamed them, and their friendship brought me back to life.

We became friends, fast.

I found that they, as a non-binary person, had unique clarity on ways to conceptualize the divine. They understood how the manifestations of the triune God can be both one thing, and another, and something so different you need new words to describe *Them* altogether.

We eventually exchanged numbers, and I gave them my actual name. That's when we realized there was something more to this story than even we knew. They'd been giving to Sub:Culture for nearly a year, after they heard me talking about its work on a podcast.

I wasn't in any rush. Neither of us were; but my feelings were changing. I googled "How to know if you're falling in love with someone?" I had never felt anything like this. How could I? I wasn't allowed to. But for the first time, I thought I understood what all the fuss was about. I didn't know where it was going; I just knew that every day was exciting and I was finally being fully myself with someone. When we finally met for our first date, the only masks we were wearing were the KN95 kind.

We both knew it would cost us everything to follow Jesus down the unfolding path of unknowing and relearning. Love was just stronger than any fear we felt. The Spirit's question about who told me I was naked started to make sense.

Nakedness is about vulnerability. It is about dependence and trust. To be vulnerable, you have to believe that nothing will hurt you or cause you harm beyond what you can handle. You have to be able to trust in a safety outside yourself, outside of your control. Someone along the way convinced us it was shameful to be naked and vulnerable, but it wasn't God.

As loved ones exited our lives in droves, it was like experiencing death and life at the same time. People claimed they loved us, but they were incapable of being happy that we were happy. We were living honestly for the first time. Living in our bodies, living in confidence, living into our authentic selves, our dignity, and our worth—for them all of that amounted to hell. The two of us knew it was the work of God leading us to love ourselves and to believe that we were loveable. This kind of safety and peace and happiness could not be from the evil one.[147] Hadn't Jesus told us that we would know a tree by its fruit?[148] The fruit here was that we both found support and a place to call home. These were the very things promised to me when I responded to altar calls at all those conferences over the years. Yet here we were, losing almost everyone in the process of finding love, and ourselves, and God again.

I had become convinced that it wasn't possible to experience the things I was experiencing in this relationship in real life, but it actually was! I had a partner, a best friend, a lover, and a confidant. I was vulnerable and unashamed.

When people found out about my queerness and my relationship, they asked if I was "wrestling with sin." The answer

147 Galatians 5:22-23; John 10:10
148 Matthew 7:15-20

was no. I was wrestling with love, and it is a far more powerful opponent. Unleavening helped me see that Jesus doesn't seem to be as obsessed with sin as we are.[149] Sin conversations are too shallow. Jesus was obsessed with love.[150] Love conversations, like the kind that fuels the kingdom of the heavens, are much more interesting.

The wilderness gave me permission to recover that which I originally loved about Jesus in the gospels and begin to live in an unleavened faithfulness. Unleavened faith embraces conviction, correction, and change—holistically and with dignity. It is about believing wholeheartedly that love is stronger than death, and that nakedness is nothing to be ashamed of. It is about acknowledging that we have the capability of causing harm, and consequently living with a consistent humble caution. It makes us take ourselves seriously enough to pay attention to our own needs and fears, so that we can be mindful of the needs and fears of others. The Jesus of the scriptures taught and demonstrated what it means to be fully human, fully alive. It is White Jesus who rejects someone for having the audacity to live an abundant life rooted in the love of God.

Nearly every conversation I had about this relationship consisted of me trying to convince people in my life to consider

---

[149] Jesus only talks about sin 16 times in the whole of the gospels. See Matthew 6:14, 12:31, 13:41; Mark 3:29; Luke 17:4; John 8:7, 11, 21, 34, 46; 9: 41; 15:22, 24; 16:8,9,11 Each of those times it is in conjunction with forgiveness. Jesus doesn't refer to the people as sinners unless he is borrowing the pharisaic term in a parable. See Luke 15:7, 10; 18:13.

[150] See: Matthew 5:43-44; Matthew 5:46; Matthew 6:5; Matthew 6:24; Matthew 19:19; Matthew 22:37; Matthew 22:39; Matthew 23:6-7; Matthew 24:12; Mark 12:30-31; Luke 6:27; Luke 6:32; Luke 6:35; Luke 7:42; Luke 7:47; Luke 11:42-43; Luke 16:13; Luke 20:13; Luke 20:46; John 5:42; John 8:42; John 13:34-35; John 14:15; John 14:21; John 14:23-24; John 14:31; John 15:9-10; John 15:12-13; John 15:17; John 15:19; John 17:26; John 21:15-17.

that I could be telling the truth about my experience, not constructing a convenient story to excuse my sinful behavior.

"I know you don't agree. I used to see it that way. I just don't anymore. I have followed Jesus to this place. Why can't, won't, don't you believe me?" I didn't need them to agree, I needed them to see.

I wanted them to look at me.

I was finally alive.

Exhibiting the Fruit of the Spirit, loving and following Jesus, and seeking to forgive and apologize for harm caused— these are not the sole possession of one gender or sexual orientation. The emphasis that unites us as the body of believers is not who we are or to whom we are attracted, but *how* we love one another.

It's the leaven of whiteness that alters our ability to recognize the fruit of Christ in people with whom we don't agree. It is that toxic infiltration that enables people to see Jesus in war, borders, segregation, greed, land theft, and violence, but not in me. Whiteness obscured the truth about me. I think this is what Jesus meant when he told the Pharisees their traditions had deceived them.[151]

White Jesus convinces us that love must look a certain way; it has to be given and received a certain way. But as I've said, true, divine love went so far as to become human so that there would always be a historical witness in case anyone ever wondered what it looked like or how to recognize it. Divine love fleshed itself out in an actual space, place, and time.[152] Things

---

[151] Mark 7:13
[152] John 1:14

change when God has ankles and eyelashes and a digestive system. If we see Jesus, we see it all, and we have no need for abstractions about who we should and should not love as siblings in Christ.

The writer of First John made it very simple. Anyone who hates a sibling in Christ is a liar if they also claim that they love God because the two are incompatible.[153] We deceive ourselves if we reject siblings in Christ with whom we disagree and call it faithfulness. Unless, of course, that faithfulness is to whiteness.

It was basic to the Pharisees' understanding of God's Law that the pious could only dine with the righteous. They criticized Jesus' participation in table fellowship, especially with those considered sinners because they understood it to be an implicit acceptance of their style of life.[154] But Jesus' actions meant they had a choice to make. They could figure out why it bothered them so much to see his love and acceptance, join his table and lose their pious status, or let the leaven lead them. God invites everyone to the table. But in the case of the Pharisees, guests forgot that it wasn't their house; they didn't prepare the food or buy it. They forgot altogether that they were *guests*, mistaking themselves for bouncers. The only thing you are supposed to do as a guest at a feast is eat. So that's what we did.

---

[153] 1John 4:20

[154] Craig Blomberg, "Jesus, Sinners, and Table Fellowship," *Bulletin for Biblical Research* 19, no. 1 (2009): pp. 35-62, http://www.jstor.org/stable/26423798.

Scars and Tables

This time when I got married, I remembered everything. Our wedding was in June at an Italian villa. We had ten guests because that's what our choice cost us. It rained in the morning for the first time in the region since December, as if God was blessing the earth again. The rain stopped right before the ceremony. The sun kissed the area where we stood, and the breeze sang the familiar song of the early days when I heard God in it. It felt special because it was my wedding day, which may sound obvious. But the fact that I could really feel it now was remarkable.

I looked beautiful. I wore a dress with a long train.

On the honeymoon I wore a two-piece to the beach with no cover-up.

I felt beautiful.

I felt.

I loved my body and myself after hating both for longer than I can remember.

After our vows, my spouse and I sat around a table with our loved ones—those who had made the choice to accept and love every part of us—feasting on delicious food and wines. And by then I had learned the real, redemptive power of a celebratory feast.

The onset of the COVID-19 pandemic changed what it meant to do church, which made it easier for me to go back. The commitment was smaller and less intimidating with virtual services. We call our weekly gathering Family Brunch, because one of the main things we do together is eat. We gather every week on Sundays, and we show our wounds, share our joys, and take communion. One person brings a Cheez-It and milk, another brioche with merlot, another a stale pretzel and reheated coffee from the day before. We eat and we drink. We bear witness and testify to the unleavened bread of abundant life. We do this in the remembrance of Jesus, a man who embodied the mystery and tension of holding space for the other. He didn't call people into a systematic theology; but he repeatedly invited people to a meal. It's no coincidence that the last thing that Jesus does with his community is celebrate a feast,[155] or that one of the first things he does after his resurrection is appear to those same people in the room where the feast took place.[156] And it is certainly no coincidence that the feast was the Passover meal, commemorating the Exodus, with no leavened bread at the table.

Then, a week later, in the same room, Jesus showed his scars to his disciple Thomas to prove that he was who he said he was: the man crucified and risen from the dead.[157] Perhaps the most redemptive thing of all on my wedding day was that I felt comfortable in my skin, even with all my scars. The things that had happened to me over the last couple decades were real; they were harmful, and they left marks. I got hurt. I was lied

[155] Matthew 26:17-19; Luke 22:7–13;Mark 14:13-16
[156] John 20:19–23; Acts 1:14; Acts 2:4
[157] John 20:27

to. I buried my pain. I flew. I tried to assert myself in fits and starts, and people I trusted punished me for it. I lost friends. I lost track of God, myself, and the point of life. You don't come out of that unscathed.

But our scars, like Jesus', tell the story of how we got to where we are—just how far God has brought us. I never saw that until I unleavened. My grief and the weight of all my experiences were always meant to be part of who I was, involved in the discernment and creativity I brought to bear on the world around me. The people at my wedding feast understood that. They knew me. And Harlym will know me. She will know love.

I will have to accept that others will continue to tell me I've changed—that they look at who I am now and don't know me anymore. It will be alright. I will sometimes be unrecognizable because of my scars.

But they are the proof of my resurrection.

Epilogue
The Crucifixion of George Floyd

I saw a bleeding brownish boy ...
The lariat lynch-wish I deplored.
The loveliest lynchee was our Lord.

—Gwendolyn Brooks[158]

It was Memorial Day, 2020. I was a single mother on food stamps sharing a spare bedroom in my parents' house with my two-year-old. It was the height of the early pandemic, so Harlym and I were talking to my grandfather through the window. He asked me how I was doing and if I was okay. I told him yes, better than ever. He asked about school. I told him I had finished my master's coursework earlier that month.

"Congratulations, Sugar!" He was the only one who called me that. Before the pandemic he would give me a twenty dollar bill to put in Harlym's savings when we came to visit. It was nice to have him so close by. His retirement home was just under ten minutes away from my parents' house.

Later that day, Officer Derek Chauvin knelt on George Floyd's neck for nine minutes and twenty-nine seconds while making an arrest over an allegedly counterfeit twenty dollar

---

[158] Gwendolyn Brooks, *Bean Eaters* (New York, NY: Harper, 1960), 32-34.

bill.[159] I thought of Pop-Pop, and how it would feel to have a knee on your neck for the whole drive to his place.

I saw the news breaking, but instead of turning to my socials and obsessing over all the details, like I had when Trayvon died, I kept playing the Fisher Price piano with Harlym. We went for a walk after that, and I thought about George. I cried for him, and Ahmaud, and Breonna, and I gave my baby girl a bath. That night, I could hear George screaming "Mama!" from the downstairs television in my parents' house. They were still watching the news.

Derek Chauvin put his left knee onto George Floyd's neck and upper back while two other officers pinned him down in the middle of his back and held his legs. For the next nine minutes and twenty-nine seconds of agony and desperation, Chauvin squeezed the life out of George Floyd in broad daylight.[160]

I didn't go downstairs to watch.

Not this time.

I didn't need to see him die for his life to matter.

I'd seen enough.

George Floyd was lynched.

Instead of pleading with white people to care or understand, I lit a candle and opened the book *Stand Your Ground* by Kelly Brown Douglas. I wept, and I read:

[159] ABC News, "George Floyd: A Man, a Moment, America Changed L 20/20 L Part 1," YouTube (ABC 20/20, April 24, 2021), https://youtu.be/VO2_gixq9ok.

[160] ABC News, "George Floyd: A Man, a Moment, America Changed L 20/20 L Part 3," YouTube (ABC 20/20, April 24, 2021), https://youtu.be/DQXI26iAKts.

The Matthean question today might be, "But Lord, where did we see you dying and on the cross?" And Jesus would answer, "On a Florida sidewalk, at a Florida gas station, on a Michigan porch, on a street in North Carolina. As you did it to one of these young black bodies, you did it to me." It is in the face of Trayvon dying on a sidewalk that we see Jesus dying on the cross. To know the extent of God's love, one must recognize the face of Jesus in the face of Trayvon.[161]

I felt the immense grief.

I felt sick to my stomach.

But I also felt God.

I was a different person, and I followed my body's lead that day. This time I had theological containers to hold what unfolded on that pavement in front of the Cup Foods in Minneapolis. BIPOC theologians and my own experience provided language for the paradox of being both Black and Christian in America. I didn't expect justice. I knew a racist backlash would come, questioning the "real" cause of his death. I had no hope that my former churches would react any way other than they always have.

But I didn't have a hard time finding God. I thought about Jesus, lynched with the permission of the state. He knew what it was to cry out to God, asking that the suffering be taken

---

[161] Douglas, Kelly Brown. *Stand Your Ground: Black Bodies and the Justice of God* Maryknoll, NY: Orbis Books, 2015. Kindle.

away, and to receive no answer. Jesus too had cried out for his mother.

Over the next week, only when I felt ready, I gathered more information about what exactly happened to Gianna's daddy. I wrote an open letter to a well-known worship leader who decided to do worship and evangelize near the site of the lynching.[162] I said it was presumptuous to think that worship was not already happening in the wailing and raging over a man in 2022 slowly killing someone with his hands in his pockets.

As I kept reading about what occurred, I fixated on the bystanders.

Donald Williams' voice played through my mind. He was from the area, and he went to Cup Foods that day just to pop in to grab something quick. He yelled at the officers.

"You could get him off the ground. You being a bum right now. You could get him off the ground, bro. You are enjoying it! Look at you. Your body language explains it you f**king bum!"[163]

Donald was joined by an EMT named Genevieve Hansen, who pleaded with them to check George's pulse.

They refused.

The two of them even moved closer and pointed out the fact that George's nose was bleeding, and that he wasn't moving.

---

[162] Marisa Iati and Sarah Pulliam Bailey, "Christian Worship Leader Brings Controversial Prayer Rallies to Cities Roiled by Protests," *The Washington Post*, September 16, 2020, https://www.washingtonpost.com/religion/2020/09/16/sean-feucht-prayer-rallies-kenosha-chicago/.

[163] ABC News, "George Floyd: A Man, a Moment, America Changed L 20/20 L Part 4," YouTube (ABC 20/20, April 24, 2021), https://youtu.be/629QZ-nfsyY.

But Chauvin threatened to mace them if they didn't get back on the sidewalk.[164]

The sidewalk.

That day the sidewalk became the foot of the cross. Darnella Frazier and her nine-year-old cousin filmed a travesty, the recording we all saw, that bore witness.[165]

I opened the scriptures and read about Rizpah.[166] Her story is lesser known, but it had been comforting when I read the previous news about Ahmaud and Breonna. Rizpah lived in a violent, patriarchal society and didn't seem to have much power. She never even speaks in the text, but her actions were beautiful. Her two sons were killed, executed in a cycle of violence that plagued Israel and Judah at the time. She couldn't bring them back or defeat the army that killed them, but she could make sure that people saw what had happened. She decides to mourn in a unique and public way that honors the loss. She leaves the bodies of the murdered on the mountainside in plain sight and sleeps on a sackcloth beside them.

Then she refuses to leave.

She shoos scavengers away and protects the bodies from wild animals. Rizpah had no meaningful power as a female concubine in her day. But she ensured that the bodies of her sons—the sons that the state slew—remained. Dignified, apparent, and indisputable in all their terror.

---

[164] *8 Minutes and 46 Seconds*, *YouTube* (Sky News, 2020), https://youtu.be/xvW6PLIDs-bI.

[165] Amy Forliti, "Teen Who Recorded Floyd's Arrest, Death Wins Pulitzer Nod," AP NEWS, June 11, 2021, https://apnews.com/article/pulitzer-prize-2021-citation-darnel-la-frazier-george-floyd-dce128319a373cf5360237f4c80dc9bb.

[166] 2 Samuel 21:1-14

That's what Darnella Frasier did with her cell phone and social media. She made sure that everyone saw.

George Floyd was crucified—despised and rejected by the state and many in his own country.

Many sympathetic white people asked, "What crime has this man committed to warrant a death like that?" but they should have already known the answer. We had been telling them for centuries. I had been telling them since Trayvon's shoes protruded from underneath that canary yellow blanket.

The answer was none.

When the story was told of what happened to the man from Nazareth, the result was liberation for the world. As the images of George Floyd made their way around the planet, in nearly every country, people sang the song of the value of Black life. *That* too is gospel.

There wasn't anything redemptive about what happened to him.

It was wicked.

Black people don't need to keep dying for white America to see its sins.

But they do.

We live in the tension of how things are and how they should be. We can join the mourning of Rizpah and, like the bystanders, become the heralds of the truth. We have a choice each day to hope even in the midst of travesty. Some of my ancestors were born, lived, and died enslaved and never dreamed that they would be free, but they fought for freedom anyway. Hope is not facile or once and for all. It is a constant struggle, and it is all that any of us can do. But it will not disappoint.

Hope will not put us to shame.

Acknowledgements

Thank you to Ellison for holding the family down while I wrote, and for the late-night editing sessions on the deck.

Thank you to the Inverse Community and my Family Brunch crew. God truly sets the lonely in family.

Thank you to Megan, Alyssa, Tabatha, and Christine for reading the pages and pages of random material I sent you at all hours of the night.

Thank you, Robert, Tamara, Nya, Sarah, Anastasia, Amber, Morgan, Erin R., Ann, Emmie, Michelle, Becca, Ashley, Erin K, and the Brandons. Your friendship over the years has added so much color and joy to my life, and consequently to these pages.

Thank you to Cami and Elyssa for letting us borrow the lake house so I could write and rest.

Thank you to the Minehart Fam for welcoming me in and teaching me.

Thank you to Suzie, Jonathan, and Sy for giving me this opportunity and believing in me.

Thank you, Mom and Dad, for your consistent reminder that Black is beautiful.

Thanks to Emily for coaching me through the process and reminding me to shine my light.

Thank you, Grace, you told me a long time ago I could do it, and you never let me forget or fight it.

Thank you to all my students and interns through the years. I do all of this for you.

The Land

Before anything was on the earth, water used
to come up from the ground to water it.

—Genesis 2:1

Earth was there. Water was there. Humanity formed from the dust of the earth, and God breathed into them life. God, people, and place were intertwined to express and explore their kinship.

My dear friend Sarah Quint asked me once if I could imagine God pulling the earthworms and the twigs out of the soil as humanity was created. I couldn't. I have always had a complicated relationship to soil. I come from a *stolen people* forced to pillage *stolen land*.

Sarah was a guide for my reintroduction to the land. The land that has cloaked hush harbor prayers, healed stripes on belabored backs, and hidden my ancestors as they sought freedom. The land that has soaked up our blood and sends its cries up through the soles of our feet and out of our mouths as we march American streets.

I am living on the lands of *her* people—Powhatan land. The Lands of the Mattaponi Tribe in Tsenacommacah, and I receive my water from the James River watershed. Sarah told me not to worry—that the trees could hear and see—that they remember my ancestor's tears. She shared a song in her mother tongue and taught me how to sing it.

Author Biography

Tamice Spencer-Helms is a published author, speaker, and theologian based in Richmond, Virginia. After 16 years of full-time ministry, she founded <u>Sub: Culture Incorporated</u>, a non-profit that provides holistic support and crisis relief for Black college students.

In addition to her bachelor's degree in Religious Studies and Copywriting, Tamice has an M.A. in Contextual Leadership and an M.A. in Theology.

Over the years, Tamice has been a change-maker and pioneer for young people in her community. Throughout her life, she has connected, supported, and ministered to countless young adults and college students. Her friendly and down-to-earth approach to public speaking and teaching, as well as her dedication to theological study, has helped empower and inspire people in her community and beyond.

Tamice lives in Richmond with her spouse Ellison, her daughter Harlym, and her puppy Beacon. In her spare time, she loves to dissect and listen to Hip-Hop, watch documentaries, savor whiskey, eat Ellison's homemade pizza, and relax with her family.